'Jan Cavelle has written a must-read primer that offers behind-the-scenes insight into the journey of fascinating and diverse business leaders who share the highs, lows and in-betweens of entrepreneurship.'

Nancy Thompson, Founder & President,
Vorticom, Inc.

'*Scale for Success* does a brilliant job of weaving together stories, lessons and thoughtful reflections. Each one of the entrepreneurs featured could write a book. Until they do, this is the one to read.'

Oli Barrett MBE, Co-Founder, StartUp Britain
and Co-Founder, Turn On The Subtitles

'Business is challenging at every level. Fortunately most of these challenges have been solved, you just need to know where to look. *Scale for Success* collates many lifetimes' worth of insights, shortcuts and wisdom. Grab a copy, take notes and get to work!'

David Jenyns, Founder, SYSTEMology

'In *Scale for Success*, Jan talks with real people as they recount their business challenges with warmth and clarity whilst revealing key takeaways. A refreshing change from the usual jargon-filled business books.'

Tara Hawkins, Director, Authentic Villa Holidays

'*Scale for Success* shows the reality of business growth as an entrepreneur. With real, frank discussion of the challenges that plague small businesses, solutions become possible.

Jan shares those stories and solutions, creating a practical guide for business at any stage.'

Nettie Owens, Founder & CEO,
Momentum Accountability

'Every year that a company survives in business should be celebrated – the tenacity to bring together essential ingredients for scaling an early stage venture should never be taken lightly. *Scale for Success* highlights these essential qualities and includes valuable references to entrepreneurs and their success stories.'

Rick Anstey, Founder, inQbator, iQFunds,
and iQ360, Queensland, Australia

'*Scale for Success* tells the stories of growth enterprise, delivers some of the essential rules of growth, and will inspire anyone that reads it. The outrageously tough journey of building a company and actually enjoying the process is very rare but Jan has captured the stories of those that have worked hard to build their success.'

Lara Morgan, Founder & Co-Owner, Scentered
and Founder, Global Amenities Direct

'What I love about this book is that Jan provides in-depth stories that truly engage and connect with the reader. This is how business books should be written.'

Joseph Meuse, Founder & President, Business GPS

'Jan has an incredible knack of making scaling applicable and accessible for entrepreneurs and start-ups. Making the human connection between real examples and applicable strategies is golden. Relatable, human, and super valuable, this is a must-read for the business owner getting ready to scale.'

Jo Gifford, Content Development Lead,
author and podcaster

scale

for

success

Expert Insights into
Growing Your Business

JAN CAVELLE

BLOOMSBURY BUSINESS
LONDON · OXFORD · NEW YORK · NEW DELHI · SYDNEY

BLOOMSBURY BUSINESS
Bloomsbury Publishing Plc
50 Bedford Square, London, WC1B 3DP, UK
29 Earlsfort Terrace, Dublin 2, Ireland

BLOOMSBURY, BLOOMSBURY BUSINESS and the Diana logo are
trademarks of Bloomsbury Publishing Plc

First published in Great Britain 2021

A catalogue record for this book is available from the British Library

Library of Congress Cataloguing-in-Publication data has been applied for

ISBN: HB: 978-1-4729-8555-2; TPB: 978-1-4729-8556-9; eBook: 978-1-4729-8558-3

2 4 6 8 10 9 7 5 3 1

Typeset by Deanta Global Publishing Services, Chennai, India
Printed and bound in Great Britain by CPI Group (UK) Ltd, Croydon CR0 4YY

To find out more about our authors and books visit www.bloomsbury.com
and sign up for our newsletters

This book is dedicated to my son, Jack, who is not just incredibly special to me, but also encouraged and supported me in writing this book. Without him, it might never have existed. In addition to that, he has left me in awe of his courage during what has been an incredibly tough year for him.

Contents

Introduction

All my life I have been an entrepreneur. I have started micro-businesses that have stayed deliberately micro and one high-growth, multi-million business. That high-growth one happened organically, a roller-coaster ride I got on and for a long while, I couldn't get off again.

This fairground ride brought me glittering opportunities. During my 20-odd years of running that business, I won regional and national business awards. I was proud to represent the UK in the European Parliament as one of 50 women to spearhead a campaign for women's enterprise; I discussed the economy on BBC Two's *Newsnight* under the kind encouragement of both Jeremy Paxman and Emily Maitlis. I debated at the Cambridge Union. Perhaps the most exciting opportunity for me was to be able to write for a variety of business publications, most notably *Real Business*. Had I bothered with any education, writing was what I had always dreamed of doing. Not too shabby for someone who started businesses originally with not one jot of knowledge and probably just as little skill.

That lack of knowledge and skill became more significant when it came to growing the business rather than starting one. I worked at remedying that ignorance by applying to become a member of a high-growth business club in London called The Supper Club. They were very selective about whom they interviewed and even more so about whom they let in. To my slight amazement, they accepted me, and for several years, I attended business dinners and training courses with some of the very best entrepreneurs in the UK. Everything we discussed was always under Chatham House rules (in which information shared can be disclosed, but the sources cannot be identified), and everyone was incredibly open about the problems they encountered in growing a business. I loved it. I never made any secret of the fact that I was a minnow among whales and no one ever seemed to mind.

They had all been where I was. I learned just what a difference it makes when you talk to someone who understands the issues you are up against from personal experience. It was a sudden feeling of belonging for the first time and I profited hugely from both that and the incredible stream of knowledge on offer. We all benefited because we really understood each other's problems – one of which was just how tough it is to scale up. I heard the same thing from the editors of the business publication *Real Business*, to which I was contributing regularly by that time. They, too, stressed how much people wanted to read real-life stories of what life is like running a small business. We all talk the same language and I am always fascinated to know what makes other entrepreneurs feel successful and what makes them succeed when they can appear to be so very different.

By chance, when I was starting to plan this book, I re-watched both the film *Rush*, telling the story of former adversaries Niki Lauda and James Hunt, and *Borg vs McEnroe*, a biographical indie film of the 1980 tennis rivalry between Björn Borg and John McEnroe. In both cases, yet in two different fields – motor-racing and tennis – you have world champions who appear to be polar opposites. Niki Lauda, a measured, controlled family man, versus playboy, devil-may-care James Hunt. Or Björn Borg, the ice-cold, ultra-controlled Swede versus the emotional, work-hard-play-hard American John McEnroe. Yet all four succeeded. Even odder, each pair ended up becoming close friends. The simple reason was that they understood each other at a very primary level. The more I have thought about this, the more I have become convinced that this is at the heart of why entrepreneurs learn most and best from other entrepreneurs. Who else can understand what drives us, especially when it is often extremely hard work and very far from the glamour that people outside assume it involves?

This book is for other aspiring stars of entrepreneurship. Some of you may be just starting, but already set on a course to scale from the get-go. Others may already be running a business, desperate to scale up but struggling to work out how to do so, as I did. Starting a business is hard and scaling a business harder. If you didn't know this, you wouldn't be reading this book. I reached the multi-million mark but couldn't sustain it and I had belated lightbulb moments while talking to virtually everyone involved in this book.

One problem with scaling is that every step is uncharted territory that we can get lost in. Another is that when we start, we are so excited about our new businesses that it is easy to bounce out of bed and go at a hundred miles an hour. It's a heady mix of fear and exhilaration, a bit like the one you get when you do adventure sports. But like that adrenaline kick from doing sports, it can be a temporary high and when it wears off, you are in trouble.

Jeremy Harbour of The Harbour Club & Unity Group nails it when he says later in the book: 'Most people start businesses for more time and more money, or because they are pissed off with someone telling them what to do. Then they find they have no time, no money, never switch off, and while it is exciting for a time, in the end, it grinds you down.'

Unless we have a source that feeds our inspiration and motivation, our enthusiasm starts to wane. And when that happens, all the obstacles that come our way seem suddenly twice the size they were yesterday. We get stuck and can't find the way forwards to take the business up to the next level. We start to panic that we are going to be stuck doing the same thing long term. And we have no idea how to change things.

The entrepreneurs interviewed in the book come from a wide variety of business sectors and from all over the world. Between them, they have many hundreds of years of entrepreneurial experience. In addition to their practical advice, they tell very relatable stories about the struggles they had, many of the same ones that you are going through right now. You can choose to read the book from start to finish, but you can also dip into or back into a particular topic you are stuck on for practical help.

The people in this book will inspire you on those days when you find yourself struggling. Read how DC Designs' Durell Coleman's family set an example for him, which has grown into a passion for helping the people whom society overlooks. Admire how Californian health entrepreneur Jeff Fenster combatted a childhood terror of cancer by becoming fascinated by nutrition. Read of the incredible Dame Shellie Hunt, born into poverty, now honoured by the Order of St John for her philanthropic achievements globally.

Discover how even James Davidson and his partners of tails. com, with some of the cream of entrepreneurial experience behind them, still came close to closure by making the nearly fatal error of concentrating on tech over customers. Or how Outland Denim's James Bartle gained, but nearly lost, from the Meghan Markle effect. And how multi-millionaire Jeremy Harbour's first two businesses both crashed so severely he had to move back in with his parents. You will come away braced by the fact that even the best of us make colossal mistakes.

When I first mapped out the concept for this book, I racked my brains for whom I knew, who had a great story to tell, or who had undergone business struggles that other people would identify with, or for those who were real, often global experts in their field. Then I added a whole lot of different names that I had heard of, which I felt would meet the same criteria. I sent messages out, asking for help.

I was utterly overwhelmed by the unqualified offers of help from incredible people, with hugely busy and successful lives. They had absolutely nothing to gain bar the knowledge that, maybe, chatting to me might mean their wisdom would reach others. This sort of generosity is typical of successful entrepreneurs in my experience, but I was still astounded by how far it went. They have all enabled me to set out the book how I originally intended. It will help you in your journey to scale, from forming a strategy, re-examining what you stand for, raising finance, nailing your sales and marketing, creating a great team, running the business and growing it from 1m to the next 5m–10m. Each of these sections has both entrepreneurs' own stories to inspire you, together with practical tips and advice on that subject and key takeaways.

You will hear from entrepreneurs in a wide variety of business sectors, some high profile, some less so, some names behind leading household brands, some niche specialists. Some are serial entrepreneurs who have sold businesses for millions, others are well established in current companies and some are early on their journeys. They are now your support team of 30 exceptional entrepreneurs. You will identify with their struggles and their wins, their tears and laughter at every stage, and they will provide invaluable support while you scale up.

Jan Cavelle

PART ONE

Planning to Scale

Even the most seasoned entrepreneur can stumble at one of the leaps up in scale. We make the mistake of assuming that the secret to scaling is doing more of what we have been doing. Much as that might sound logical, it doesn't work out that way.

No one knows better than I that it is entirely possible to grow a business up to around the £1m turnover mark by selling, anything, everywhere to anyone. I went way past that by running a lifestyle business from the kitchen table at home but there are all sorts of reasons why that is not sustainable as you grow further.

Growing further will involve bringing more people on to your team, inspiring them and communicating with them. It will require structures that work to deliver more of what you were doing before in a consistent way. You may well need finance. It requires a whole new approach to sales and marketing, as you cannot grow sales sufficiently to scale in the more-the-merrier haphazard approach that small-scale businesses often depend upon. All of this needs planning. In the following two chapters, both James Bartle and Bev Hurley share how being unprepared for growth caught them unawares. Bev delves further into what you need to do in order to scale while James explains how purpose makes growth easy and why he believes a strong purpose has become a business essential. A purpose is often deeply embedded in our values and in Chapter 5, Nicole Lamond shares how her entire business is built around her values and the advantages of that. We have all heard that we need to find our passion, our personal motivation, but how do we find it practically? In Chapter 4, Durell Coleman shares the process he uses personally and argues that what you do is immaterial in comparison to the reason you do it.

Finally, strategy. The core element of scaling. Stephen Kelly, currently chair of Tech Nation, is a true global expert. Starting his career at Oracle, Stephen was CEO of Sage, Micro Focus, and Chordiant during their growth years. He talks of why the leap between 1–10m is so often the 'Death Valley of Scaling Up' and how to survive it.

Your Vision and Mission

James Bartle, Outland Denim

JAMES'S STORY

James Bartle grew up in a remote Australian community. His parents were pastors and he regularly lost his bed to someone in need. James remembers his mum getting grief from a drunk guy and how she dealt with it with so much grace and compassion. He was a shy child and that sometimes held him back from speaking out for those in need, but he was always compassionate.

James did a traineeship in business just after he left school but never intended to be an entrepreneur, unless 'you count mowing lawns and things'. He was a freestyle motocross athlete and had a small metal fabrication business. By chance, he watched the Liam Neeson film *Taken* and was appalled by the human trafficking statistics at the end. He kept on thinking of his two young nieces and started to learn more about it.

James went to South East Asia with a rescue agency and saw a girl, only about 11 years old, for sale. He could see her terror, yet the agency said there was nothing they could do for her.

He learned that young girls were being sold everywhere, for sex and hard labour in mines and factories. James could see that the root of the problem was poverty. He didn't want to fundraise but instead decided to work towards changing the cause by setting up a business to give the girls respectful employment.

Living off his previously established metal fabrication business, James spent five years developing a sustainable business model. He did anything he could to raise cash, even cooking and selling sausages, but doing whatever it took. At first, he set up a non-profit, but failed to get sufficient funding and so had to transition to a for-profit model. At the end of five years, the project was helping the women in Cambodia with new lives, and they had beautiful jeans and a sustainable brand.

Rescue agencies refer women to Outland Denim in Cambodia. These women learn to be seamstresses at a fair, living wage, but are also enabled to take control of their lives. They are paid to attend lessons, learning English, how to manage their finances and especially how to get out of debt, which nearly always caused their situation.

The women's health course taught the benefits of breastfeeding. This was necessary as, years before, a marketing campaign from a baby formula company had convinced many mothers in South East Asia that buying expensive formula was a better option for their babies. Due to poverty, many were unable to afford the formula and had to use water that might be contaminated. By the end, all the staff knew the truth about breastfeeding.

James also learned of how other garment factories were polluting the streams children used for drinking. In response, Outland Denim developed stand-alone washing and finishing facilities, where their denim is finished using industry-leading water- and energy-reducing technology. Garments are dyed responsibly with only vegetable, organic dyes or dyes tested to ensure they are free from harmful chemicals.

They started marketing via influencers. James says it created brand awareness but resulted in few sales. Paid-for recommendations are no longer a good fit for the current market, which demands transparency and honesty. He finds community marketing much more effective.

The game-changer for Outland Denim came suddenly in 2018. They had launched in Canada and Australia. James had just arrived in Cambodia on a two-week trip. The first morning, his social media and phones were all going crazy. Meghan Markle had just stepped off a plane wearing their jeans. World media was going crazy and sales went through the roof. He had to fly back immediately to cope with the press conferences.

James says it was an overwhelming and emotional experience that brought them credibility, brand awareness and led to the hire of 46 more women in Cambodia. But there was a downside: a year of instability followed. He was still green and the growth was extremely rapid; they were fighting to meet orders. They had just opened a new facility in Cambodia and the culture got lost in the expansion. They had to work hard to return it to the loving and respectful ways they had previously.

Despite the fact that James had no prior fashion experience, Outland Denim became a top-end global jeans label. The drive towards their mission is what has helped them endure. James always asks himself 'how hard can it be?' and looks for a way through.

They have met plenty of challenges. Finance is always a challenge when you scale. Covid-19 brought another test, when New York closed down just at the moment when James had opened in Nordstrom's flagship store. Another huge learning curve was the cultural differences when they first started in Cambodia. James learned that when instructions result in nods, that is a gesture of respect and doesn't necessarily mean that the instructions have been understood. Relationships are currency there. It is chaos, yet they get through because they respect each other. James considers that because of this, they are more advanced than we are in other countries. He describes the people of Cambodia as 'brilliant, incredible and smart'.

James's plans for the future include involving wholesalers more to get brand exposure, pushing more into digital and to change the fashion cycles. Showing smaller ranges, more often, would mean less waste at the end of each season. They are also starting to manufacture for other brands – the first being Karen Walker.

James's definition of personal success: *'Being able to achieve the objective of influencing the industry for good and eliminate exploitation. Also, to achieve a balance of work and family relationships. My walk with my six-year-old today was interrupted by constant urgent calls and I don't want my family to sacrifice time with their dad. I want both sides to get what they need. Ideally, I want my time and space, but I am not sure if it is possible at the moment, maybe in my 50s or 60s.'*

VISION AND MISSION

Vision and mission statements are a part of virtually every business course now. What they are exactly and what their function is still confused by many business owners. By definition, a vision statement should describe what you want to achieve, your overall ambition for your business. A mission statement describes what you do, who does it and how you do it currently. Unlike a vision, a mission may change. Both statements too often end up being irrelevant and ineffective, more of a marketing tool than something arising from gut and emotion.

James and his company are a powerful force aiming at having a massive impact. Yet, when I spoke to him about mission and vision statements, he says that putting together these sorts of things is something they are bad at. Initially, this struck me as an anomaly. I wondered how such a purpose-driven company could not be shouting vision and mission statements from the rooftops. Then I realized that even at first contact with the company, you are left in no doubt about what they are aiming to do.

They do have some powerful straplines on their website. Their story starts with 'denim to end poverty', their crowdfunding page talks of 'made on purpose' and the mission is made inclusive of their customers with, 'Today, my jeans are creating social justice'.

I asked James for his definition of vision and mission. He strips the concept back and defines vision as the target of what you are trying to achieve, the 'where I want to be'. Then, he says, you add your 'why', the reason you want to get there. This 'why' is what gives it guts and the two together provide you with purpose. When you have a purpose-led company, you have one that is super-charged. You become focused on your target and not bothered about the direction you take to get there. Missions become interchangeable, and somewhat immaterial, provided that you are heading towards the vision. Focusing on purpose makes challenges far less critical.

James sometimes talks to entrepreneurs and asks them why they do what they do. When they say that they're in it for the money, he thinks, 'That isn't going to keep you going.' Others say that they are doing it to make a difference, but when he asks for more detail, they aren't sure exactly what they mean.

A vision or purpose is what gets you out of bed.

I asked James if companies about to scale should go out and try to find a purpose and a mission. He says that there is always a mission in there. You have to discover it. It may be as simple as providing for your family, and that is OK, but then you also need to help the people who work for you to find and achieve their reasons and missions, too. James believes that life is about loving one another and he is not sure why so many of us find it hard to accept people who are different.

Your vision is, therefore, always about the impact you will have on others, changing their lives or improving our planet. James believes that impact has to come through a product or a service. He also advises that you need to be very clear on how that is going to have an impact, what the concept is, how you are creating it. It has to be meaningful. You can create a social, economic or environmental impact in the community and the workplace. The whole vision then becomes part of the product and the product part of the vision.

This circle, I realize, is why there is no need to see a statement to understand Outland Denim. The customers buy into it, literally. When you buy a pair of jeans, you create an impact. Fashion has a vast ecosystem and capacity to make an impact, and brands can achieve a great deal. James's dream is to eradicate poverty and encourage purpose, not just in Cambodia, but also in other areas worldwide with similar socio-economic problems.

James says that people buy in because they too have a desire to impact for good. We all want our lives to have some meaning and make a difference. He believes our job as leaders is to help each person find their own meaning. He never micromanages but instead lets the whole team take the wins and have the pride.

What happens when you have a vision and a purpose-led company is that the staff buy in at a very different level. James speaks with warmth and admiration of a lady in Cambodia who no longer lives under a piece of plastic, has bought her own house and has paid to get her sister out of slavery. He speaks of his Australian team, whose reaction to tough conversations at the start of the Covid-19 crisis was to ask to do without their pay if it meant the vision continued and the women in Cambodia could receive theirs. That is what real buy-in to a mission looks like.

James is unusually positive about challenges and believes that you can develop resilience from having this clarity and strength of purpose. It gives you the grit to cope with the challenges and get better, and results in a close-knit, resilient team. You will never get resilience without the hurdles. Success takes hard work and dedication. James believes that too often, people run in business when times get tough. It took him 10 years from starting the research and development stage to getting to where he is now, and there were many people along the way who told him to give it up. He believes we have to change the way we talk and become more accepting of not succeeding at every challenge, and concentrate on the reason for keeping going.

James stresses that his team are strong in their own right. However, his passion for what he is aiming at is evident; he has total commitment and it shines through in everything he says. This integrity comes from genuine, natural belief in what you are doing.

James believes that any business that does not shift to having a real purpose and proper economic sustainability will become dust within 10 years. Equally, he believes that almost anyone can pivot and learn. He explains that it is the customers themselves who are changing the climate and changing it fast. It is up to brands to set prices that are right so that consumers will be able to afford to buy into the missions and be a part of a positive impact.

You need to decide if you want to be part of the problem or part of the solution. For James, owning a company is about creating change, not about having a business.

Key takeaways:

- Your vision is where you want to be and why you want to get there;
- Concentrate on the vision and missions become merely a route to getting there;
- All businesses need to adapt to be genuinely sustainable and purpose led.

2

What Makes a Business Ready to Scale?
Bev Hurley, YTKO

BEV'S STORY

I first met Bev Hurley many years ago when she was organizing a dinner for female entrepreneurs in Cambridgeshire. Not knowing what she was like or who was going to be there, I walked into the hotel bar with some trepidation. It was a busy hotel, the bar was crowded and I had no idea how to find anyone. Just as I was considering doing a runner, this figure dashed over to me, enveloped me in a hug and told me that I looked in need of a huge drink. This proved to be Bev and she was so unexpectedly warm that I instantly relaxed and settled in to enjoy myself.

Bev's genuine care for others is at the very heart of her success. She has helped thousands of women and disadvantaged groups across Britain. She is a serial entrepreneur, a Business Angel (start-up investor) and one of Britain's leading authorities on small businesses.

Bev was born in Doncaster, educated in Bedford and took both a BA and MA in science at the Open University in London. Her first job was working with a social landlord in deprived parts of the Inner City of London, working to modernize both the organization and its nineteenth-century housing stock. She speaks highly of her boss, who she says, 'let me make mistakes and try new things'. Bev created one of the first tenants' associations in London and managed the long waiting lists for homes, also carrying out a major renovation on more than 3,000 homes. It was her first exposure to poverty and disparity, and the experience was to spark a lifelong fight to create equality and opportunity.

She left to start her first business, buying up a run-down property and converting it into flats. She then sold this business to move to Canada with her new husband. A second home in Canada took them to the extreme cold, where temperatures of -40°C (-40°F) were not uncommon. She worked briefly for Noranda in Bathurst, then as an estate agent, and had her daughter. They next moved to the new Hemlo gold mine as part of their strategic team. Hemlo was 400km (250 miles) from any city. Bev describes it as being a mini Klondike once the geologists finally discovered the mother lode, with a mill making gold on site. She was part of the team that achieved such a fantastic safety record, low staff turnover and record gold production that they were able to operate union free during that period.

Returning to the UK, she and her husband split and she went back to setting up businesses while being a single mum. These included an interior furnishings business, a professional mediation company and an industrial design agency.

In 2000, Bev joined the YTKO Group as its CEO. By 2015, the Group had passed into her sole control. YTKO supports enterprise creation and business growth in both the public and private sectors across the UK and Bev has launched a stream of innovative products and services into both, Norfolk Network, Enterprising Women and GetSet for Growth among them. She believes trusting your team is at the heart of maintaining a great culture so that they feel part of what is going on. I asked her to share her advice on tendering, something many business owners fear.

'Formal procurement, tendering, getting into supply chains and so on can be a great way to grow your business,' she says. 'But it takes time to build your stock of policies, to be able to describe and differentiate yourself effectively, and often a lot of time to write the tender. In the public sector, in particular, you need to be as certain as you can be beforehand that you're not just being asked to quote to give them the mandatory three responses. It's a numbers game.'

In 2006, Bev launched a non-profit social mission across the UK that aimed to support more than 20,000 businesses, help them raise £50m to sustain and scale, and enable 10,000 new jobs to be created for the UK economy. It has already surpassed all three targets and she is especially proud that half of their clients are women. It also earned her a CBE.

I asked her what the most significant weaknesses she sees in early-stage businesses are. She says that 'by a country mile, it is the lack of understanding and use of the four essential components of an effective marketing strategy (segmentation/ prospect knowledge, cost of acquisition, differentiation and value proposition). This lack of understanding inevitably results in a waste of money on the wrong tactics and wrong message via the wrong channels. Marketing must drive business development and sales, and in the UK, we're not very good at all at this core commercial function. As a result, businesses have no idea how long it is going to take them to achieve profitability. Cash flow yo-yos and funders don't want to lend because of the risk.'

To succeed in business, Bev says you need 'mental and physical stamina, creativity and imagination, dogged determination, focus, the ability to listen, being comfortable with risk and uncertainty, the ability to acknowledge and celebrate achievements, and try always to walk the walk.'

Bev's definition of personal success: *'To disrupt markets successfully through a relentless dual focus on unmet needs and innovation, and working (and playing) with a great bunch of talented, passionate people to do so. Success is about achieving our mission and empowering and enriching our people.'*

WHAT MAKES A BUSINESS READY TO SCALE?

I asked Bev to offer her advice on what makes a business scalable and when and how to achieve it.

'Scaling up,' she explained, 'is a familiar jargon term in business with no magic meaning other than generally preparing for and executing sustainable and profitable growth. Initially, it was more frequently attached to equity-backed companies, presumably on the false assumption that if you have lots of money, fast/global business expansion is a given. Now, it is used more widely for all businesses looking to grow.

Ambition for growth and achieving it, at whatever size and stage of the journey, are two very different things. In the UK, 99.3 per cent of SMEs have fewer than 50 staff. What makes any company scalable is the ability to identify a significant unmet market need and supply a product or service that satisfies that need better than the competition. The bigger the market need, the more you will be able to sell to meet it, and therefore the more likely and sustainable your scalability will be.

One way to approach this is by finding niches and market segments where you have the best fit and have the most significant competitive advantage. Then, highly effective marketing, business development and sales are the essential strategic business functions that enable you to capitalize on those opportunities and grow your market share.

Scale-up opportunities can come at any time, so the most important thing is to pre-prepare. Bev told me about the first time YTKO doubled in size from 20 to 40 employees in a matter of weeks; they were not remotely ready. They had neither got the tech infrastructure or full HR processes and policies in place, nor had their management time or capability to cope with inducting and embedding the new people well. Instead of growing, they had to stop the business development for several months and put these things right before moving forwards again. When they suddenly doubled again a year later to 80 people, everything went more smoothly because the foundations were in place and they could concentrate on keeping the momentum going.

Bev advises that the best way to test your preparation is to imagine getting a whole year's turnover tomorrow and working through what you would have to do to prepare. This exercise will reveal any gaps that need fixing, with sufficient working capital nearly always appearing at the top of the list. To grow fast, you will need increased working capital. You will have to pay for recruitment costs, new team salaries, stock, equipment, software and cover the salaries of non-revenue-generating people like IT, finance and HR staff who will also be needed as you grow. If you can protect your intellectual property (IP), so much the better.

She went on to observe that, of course, as all business owners know, it is incredibly tough at the top, bearing all the pressure and stress, and these all grow as you scale. A key ingredient to success is to have started to build a senior team. By yourself, you might be able to directly line-manage a dozen people, but beyond that figure, it is impossible to do well. You will need two or three key people whom you trust absolutely to empower, share the load and to become co-drivers by your side, strengthening the business resilience of your company. Having an independent board with outside wisdom and experience can bring invaluable help to your growth and support and guide you personally. You need to concentrate on becoming an inspiring leader, hold on to your vision, communicate it, walk the talk and enthuse your people to come with you.

It all takes time. A board is easier to attract if you can demonstrate your business growth potential and secure equity funding. Investors will often want to take a seat on the board to help their investment reap the rewards through increasing shareholder value – yours and theirs. Investing in an experienced mentor who has been there and done it, who has 'got the scale-up T-shirt', can also bring much value to you as you go through the early stages of growth and start to build these essential people resources.

Growth always means change: for you your business and your people. The pressure increases, but so do the rewards for everyone.

Key takeaways:

- Prepare before, not during, scaling;
- It is only possible through nailing your marketing;
- Build a management team of at least two right hands first.

3

Strategy

Stephen Kelly, Chair of Tech Nation

Stephen Kelly is currently chair of Tech Nation, the champion of digital and technology scale-ups companies. He is the former chief executive (CEO) of Sage, Micro Focus and Chordiant, business ambassador for the UK prime minister and on the Top 500 UK Power List.

He was born into what he describes as a working-class background, attending the local state school in Folkestone, a poor seaside town with few jobs. His parents had lived through the Second World War, with his father away serving in Burma and India. They impressed their values on Stephen and he lives by them still: to do right by people, do an honest day's work, hard work never hurt anyone, treat others as you wish to be treated yourself. Following the war, his father sold tea and coffee to local restaurants and life revolved around the business, with Stephen helping out in the shop after school. There was a blur between home and business. If one of the restaurants his father supplied had run out of something, it was never a problem for his father to deliver at the weekend. Customers and their happiness were at the heart of everything. Stephen learned to be authentic and make customers his friends.

The first in his family to go to university, Stephen studied business administration at the University of Bath. In only his second job, he joined Oracle's European management team. Out of their 12 years to that point, they had tripled growth in 11 of those years. He describes Oracle as being addicted to growth. Stephen learned that in business you need to 'grow fast or die slowly'. He also learned the essential ingredients to run high-scaling companies, which, he says, come down to doing the simple stuff well. Oracle's policy was to hire an exceptional, over-experienced team, well in advance of their needs. At £12m turnover, they would hire someone who had built £100m businesses.

Stephen's childhood, combined with his time with Oracle, is the foundation of his statement that he has scale-up growth embedded in his DNA. In 1997, he joined a California-based start-up called Chordiant as its new CEO. It grew rapidly, raising $70m in revenue in four years. They went from VC (venture capital) private backing to become one of NASDAQ's leading customer relationship management companies with a significant increase in revenues and market value, and joined the Deloitte Fast 50.

Stephen says that in California he learned what a white-knuckle roller-coaster ride it can be as a founder and how it can be a hugely emotional experience, too. There are many dark days as you swing between massive highs and lows when you have failed to deliver. As a leader, you must remain calm and reflective – your team is focused and empowered by their journey towards the North Star, while your own emotions are see-sawing in turmoil.

In California, he also learned how important it is to plan to be the market leader. Market leaders win in spades and get the spoils. Those who come second are viable and the rest just pick up scraps, pre-acquisition. Massive consolidation is especially true in tech, with companies like Amazon, Oracle and Google. All were relentless on growth and becoming market leaders; they were Darwinian on domination.

Stephen says he has 'stepped on the shoulders of giants'. At Oracle, he worked under titans of leadership Marc Benioff, Dr Steve Garnett and Polly Sumner (Dr Garnett has remained his mentor for more than 30 years). They have been there to tap him on the shoulder and encourage him to try new things when opportunities have arisen throughout his career. From them, Stephen learned that one individual can build much success for others. Seeing others exceed their potential is Stephen's primary motivation – it has never been about money.

On his return from California eight years later, Stephen became CEO of the FTSE software firm Micro Focus International, tripling revenues, growing in value from £180m to £1bn worth in three years and leading them to become a Top 200 UK public company. He also joined the UK government as COO of the Civil Service under Cabinet Minister Francis Maude. He was then appointed the prime minister's business ambassador and was tasked with helping to boost the UK's international trade performance, a post he remained in until 2018.

Stephen became CEO for the software giant Sage in 2014. Sage saw its market value double and a shareholder return of more than twice that of the FTSE 100. He is particularly proud of launching the Sage Foundation, helping the vulnerable and disadvantaged in the community, giving people a chance of a better life.

In June 2020, Stephen was appointed chair of Tech Nation, which he describes as a fabulous business under the brilliant leadership of Gerard Grech. Tech Nation's network includes seriously fast-growing tech companies: Monzo, Deliveroo, Revolut, Babylon. The focus is all on growth, with coaching for CEOs and senior management and fantastic content in terms of reports.

Almost 10 per cent of people now work within the tech economy. Tech Nation wants to spawn a fantastic new generation of unicorns (a start-up with a value of more than $1 billion) and scale-ups, creating 200,000 jobs. By 2030, up to 50 per cent of the economy will be in digital, tech and creative industries. They plan to fight the economic downturn and job losses from the pandemic by thinking 'Big for Britain'. With the onset of the global pandemic, the world has changed. GPs are conducting video appointments and grandparents are telling bedtime stories via WhatsApp. Within times of human tragedy, there are always opportunities and innovation. Crashes and recessions have seen giants such as Uber, Airbnb, Inc. SalesForce.com and Microsoft emerge. Stephen believes there is an opportunity for collaboration between the private sector and the UK government to create prosperity, high-value jobs and the levelling of regions.

We can't be first in everything, but Stephen wants us to lead or be second in certain areas, including Healthtech, EdTech, Lawtech, Fintech, AI and net zero. Fintech in the UK was already the second-biggest investment destination, beating China in 2019.

Anyone with a successful career has to make balances and sacrifices. Stephen pays tribute to his 'brilliant partner', Siobhan, saying he could not have done it without her. When people see the greats, such as Bezos, Branson, Jobs, they don't see the personal sacrifices that have gone on behind the success. They don't see the Sunday evenings spent on flights to New York, or the lost magical times with the children. Stephen says he loves life and being alive and part of a vibrant community, but we can't create more time. He wants to spend his time building something special for both customers and employees. Inevitably, when you put your heart and soul into something, you struggle to switch off. He becomes consumed by guiding a team, waving the flag to the top of the mountain. That means making sacrifices.

Stephen's definition of personal success: It is '*through growth, company and personal growth. Customers, persever-ance, drive and seeing progression are my guiding lights, combined with the beauty of seeing people achieving and building sustainable cultures that create a legacy after you have left the company.*'

A STRATEGY FOR SCALING

Stephen has scaled NASDAQ and both FTSE 250 and 100 companies, but there is what he calls the Death Valley to cross first, before success – the leap between 1m and 10m. In Death Valley, many die off, while others revert to being lifestyle companies.

Stephen says the first of the two largest dangers in Death Valley is founder's syndrome. Some CEOs respond poorly to the challenges while others let their egos and their attachment to pet projects get in the way of company good. Others fail to give people around them the space to grow and take the company forwards. A leader's primary role is to serve and build something magical for customers, teams and, ultimately, the shareholders and community. They need to set a culture where people thrive, which means coaching, developing and sometimes having tough conversations. Many are too afraid of failure. They need a balance of humility and fearfulness. When Carol Realini, the founder of Chordiant, interviewed Stephen, she said it would have been great if he had experienced a few failures. Failure is seen as part of the learning and development process there.

Stephen talks of how Larry Ellison, co-founder, CTO and executive chairman, created a ground for outstanding people at Oracle, enabling them to transition from founders to CEOs, which requires a different mindset. Chaos has to be in the past. CEOs need to drive value for customers and their teams. Leaders have to be able to communicate transparently, now more than ever, and do so often, both formally and informally. They need to develop empathy, especially over mental health issues. They need to bind everyone with a customer obsession and building robust systems that provide value.

Three things define a great leader: decisiveness, prioritization and bringing a team with you. Stephen refers to both team and customers as colleagues and says they should be galvanized by your magical vision, becoming your best advocates. Whether that creating a better world, innovating for tomorrow or simply meeting customer needs, your vision has to have everyone jumping out of bed with excitement at 5 a.m. every morning.

Stephen believes in setting the 'tone at the top' for a culture with authenticity and integrity. People need to connect to both the vision and their leader. The tone must enable everyone to be comfortable to be their authentic selves, which means total diversity. It must help and inspire people to become the best version of themselves. They should be going home on a Friday saying, 'I made a difference this week.' This tone results in a culture of meritocracy and one that is open to feedback. Stephen feels that in the UK, we are reluctant to give honest feedback. We need to accept perfection isn't possible and concentrate on doing our best, both as leaders and teams. Rigorous feedback, someone once told him, is the breakfast of champions. It creates an invigorating culture where you and your team can both look positively at your journey and see how you have improved, then raise quality and output by discussing mistakes and what you can do differently.

Stephen agrees with the world-famous management consultant Peter Drucker's quote, 'Culture eats strategy for breakfast.' Aim for a culture of flawless execution, a quick retro feedback loop. What results is a vibrant culture where people want to work for you, be part of your business and hunker down for a long time. Enjoy people and have fun.

The second key to making it across Death Valley lies in organizational readiness. You need to grow a quality team of senior people capable of taking the early success forwards and making it sustainable. That means finding people with the right skills and experience but who are still willing to learn and have a great attitude. Team performance and morale can be one of the CEO's worst headaches. Those people join because of your vision of future rewards. Stephen describes how the president of Oracle, Ray Lane, set out his vision to early executives and how it would result in a five-fold stock increase. When early members have equity, it becomes their company and they become incentivized.

A CEO should spend a lot of their time hunting out strong people, both as individuals and as team players. Use your network and take up references scrupulously. Stephen is less bothered about cultural fit as he believes that outstanding people find common ground in their merits. Talent trumps strategy. Forming a core executive team with the capability to adapt, win and drive the rest of the team is critical. A-class strategy and B-class execution will lose out to a B-class strategy and A-class execution every time.

Another key to survival is to make money before you raise it. Don't get obsessed with reaching your perfect product at the start. Settle for a MVP (minimal viable product) to keep revenue coming in. Avoid raising money against your home, or using credit cards for growth. Funding should be a drip-feed process. Time spent on first-round, friends-and-family-round financing can be kept to a minimum if you have a clear value, proposition and plan.

Angels often need only a couple of meetings and take minimal due diligence but bring not only money but also expertise contacts. Try to find one from your industry so they know the particular pitfalls. Set a £50k minimum level of investment to simplify shareholder management issues later on and reward those early investors for taking the risk. Consult a good accountant in advance for maximum tax efficiency.

VCs only go ahead with a small percentage of the companies they do due diligence on, yet during that time all the CEO's focus is on keeping them happy, not the business, and that is dangerous. Another danger is that some boards are formed for an exit. A focus on exiting destroys growth, with short-term thinking.

Raising money can be dangerously distracting for a CEO, but so too are continual cash-flow worries. If you drip-feed investment as needed every 18 months or two years, creating a cash runway, the CEO is free to concentrate on the critical things – the customers, his team and innovation. Each round should bring more support to the CEO.

Funding should cover all growth, hiring, sales, marketing and product. During this stage, 80 per cent of costs are likely to be employee related, so recruitment is doubly critical. Offering equity can also attract quality hires at under-market-level salaries. Plan conservatively, but be aware that over-funding makes waste too easy. Preserving cash must be an essential part of a company's DNA. Cash is the fuel of growth.

If you focus on growth and profit, you create momentum and it happens. When you focus on your customers, sales happen. Focus on making your product something that will transform people's lives and of compelling value and it will sell. Delight your customers and you will grow.

Ensure your customers develop a strong dependency on you. Empathize with them, talk to them, work with them for the long term. Stephen suggests creating a cross-functional team focused on how you can become irreplaceable, with people from sales, marketing and finance.

Stephen loves to build companies with authenticity at their heart and fulfil the two critical stakeholder briefs, having your customers and team at the heart of everything. Doing this means being out in the trenches with the troops and your customers. There, you learn what your customers need today but also what they will need from you tomorrow.

Ensure everyone loves the company and becomes a brand advocates, be it your team or your customers. Lead from the front with energy and persistence and concentrate on just four things: winning customers, retaining them, building your perfect product and hiring the best. Ensure both the founder and the organization are ready and able for success.

Stephen remains obsessed with growth, with customers and high-performance culture. 'If you put your employees and your customers on each side, you have the two sides of a perfect coin. The right culture puts the customer at the heart of the business and that is the start of success,' he says.

Key takeaways:

- Create a culture with coaching and developing where people thrive and are brand advocates;
- Concentrate your time on recruiting the right people for organisational readiness to grow;
- Drip-feed investment so that you are never over-funded, but never distracted by under-funding.

4

Designing Lasting Businesses
Durell Coleman, DC Designs

DURELL'S STORY

Durell Coleman's parents set a model of what he hopes to become and how he hopes to live his life. He describes them as two of the elements. His mother was the wind. No height was too tall, no distance too long. She had a million ideas before breakfast and made things happen, with seemingly no resources or in places where others would have quit. His father was the waves, a sea that had crashed on to the beaches for millions of years. He was methodical, persistent and did more before lunch than most people will do in their whole day. Both of them had grown up poor and taught Durell to persevere, overcome challenges by making decisions and believe that anything is possible if you are willing to put in the work. The family motto was 'never give up'.

Durell told his grandmother he would one day have his own business when he was four. He wanted to be an inventor and create flying cars. But when Durell was nine, tragedy struck and his elder brother was diagnosed with cancer. Before he died, he challenged Durell to improve cancer treatments.

Durell changed direction, deciding inventions had no value unless they helped people.

He won a place at Stanford to study mechanical engineering. His professor asked him to list 100 problems he would like to solve in the world. Durell told me that early on the list he had things such as his clothes not drying thoroughly or the cracks in the sidewalk bothering him when he skateboarded. By item number 67, he had stopped thinking of himself and had started thinking about the things that used to get to him. Number 67 was poverty. He wishes more entrepreneurs would innovate to address the hurricanes that come every year, destroying property, ending lives, or wildfires in the Amazon and Australia.

Durell shifted his focus to designing solutions to these problems. He went back to Stanford to do an MA in sustainable design, hoping to develop a wind turbine for developing countries. He says that it failed when he stopped talking to the people he was trying to help. Difficult though that was, it taught him a lot and made him even more determined to focus on human-centred design as opposed to just data.

He went through Stanford's start-up accelerator programme, StartX, a second time for Project Spark. Spark, he says, taught him a lot about what not to do in running a business. DC Design became a contract product design and prototyping business. It took five years to get the company stable.

By 2015, they had diversified too much and regrouped to focus on Durell's original aim of tackling social problems. They launched their award-winning Design the Future Design Thinking and STEM summer programme to teach high school students to design products that improved the lives of people with disabilities. Using the techniques they had developed to identify problems, they created better solutions.

The challenges they now tackle are diverse. Some examples include working with refugees in Syria, low-income communities in Miami, or on the US foster care system in Silicon Valley. They develop and implement strategies for reducing jail recidivism, consulting architects, physicians and nurses on designing optimal emergency departments. They work with foundations, non-profits and governments, wherever there are people affected by the flaws in the American social system, be they poverty, health or inequality. Durell wants to help those who can't do what they want in life because systems don't work.

The company always works with the people affected rather than raw data. Working like this enables them to identify where the real issues lie, approach them with respect and empathy and achieve better results. They give people both a voice and the value they deserve, and as a result, those people become open to change.

DC Design is a profit-making organization, which forces them to be efficient and find stable, market-ready ways to meet the needs of those who most need help. They keep their core small, using contractors to scale up as needed on different projects. Durell believes there are two sides to how we change the world around us. One is that we redesign systems so that they work better for everyone, remembering that everything started as a design and we should be continually optimizing them. The second thing to recognize is that there are aspects of ourselves that need to be redesigned. We need to focus and work on both. Durell's North Star has always been that he wants 'to be the catalyst for the realization of ambition'.

Durell lectures at Stanford and a PBS documentary, *Extreme by Design* (2013), featured his work and is now a teaching aid all over the world. He was awarded a Jefferson Award for Public Service in 2018.

Durell's definition of personal success: It is, he says, best summed up in his favourite quote from the American humourist Erma Bombeck: *'When I stand before God at the end of my life, I would hope that I would not have a single bit of talent left and could say I used everything you gave me'.* He then used his own words to further explain: *'knowing I have done everything I could to be the best version of myself that I could possibly be, and I know the best version of me is someone who helps other people see and realize their potential.'*

DESIGNING LASTING BUSINESSES

I asked Durell if the vision and mission statement is the starting point for starting or scaling businesses. He told me that he finds it extremely difficult to sum up what they do in a few words. What is much more important for any entrepreneur is that they follow their North Star.

When you are the founder of a business and you are putting your fire, passion, energy and vision into something that perhaps no one else can see, you need to be clear on what your mission is, what you stand for, what matters to you and what doesn't. Then you can guide your business instinctively.

Businesses without any purpose may advance you in many ways in life, perhaps financially or socially, or by providing external validations of power, money and fame. They will not authentically advance you or give you a feeling that you have achieved something that truly matters. That business may last five, 10 years, but you, the entrepreneur, will not be advancing in any way you genuinely yearn to do. At DC Design, they help people self-actualize and follow their passion. It can be hard to find your North Star and Durell kindly shared with me the process he teaches and applies himself.

When we are small, people ask what we want to be when we grow up – a lawyer, fireman, perhaps. They talk of titles, but not of the impact you will have. The same thing happens in college. We pick courses without asking why.

Any choice you make in life should always start with why. Instead, we use emotional decision making, in the moment and based on limited information, choosing careers or businesses we stay in for years and letting that choice define us. The North Star approach sets a destination, working out what you want to do when you get there and basing all your other decisions on how to get there.

To work out your North Star, ask yourself what brings you joy in life and write the answers down. It might be the beach or the TV, or family games, or championing causes. On a second sheet, list what makes you angry in life. Often, we avoid looking at these, which is what causes so much anger under the surface in people. Circle the five most important things, then underline the top three. Finally, star the top one.

Now write down your goals for both, one that will bring you maximum joy and one to reduce the tension that makes you angry. Give those top two time periods, one, five and 15 years. Write down as many goals for each period as you can, ending by selecting your top ones in the same way. If you then always focus on the 15-year one, you will create a life that cultivates your joy and dissipates the anger. You can, and should, revisit and recalibrate to check if you feel the same and your life is still in line. Always be clear where your business is going and why it matters to you.

As entrepreneurs, we will often question if what we are doing is worth it and if we are going about it the right way to be successful. It takes unquantifiable amounts of energy to go through the whole process. Durell says it isn't that we can't get there, more that some people believe the energy level required is too high. Following a North Star means you know where you are going in life no matter what, that you are going to get there, and when you get knocked down, you will get back up again. If you don't, you will get into trouble. Knowing where you want to go gives you an unlimited source of fuel to face the next challenge.

For developing and testing a business and business idea for long-term sustainability, Durell utilizes the design-thinking process. He learned this at Stanford and elements of this process have been used by innovators and entrepreneurs from Thomas Edison, Henry Ford and Jonas Salk to Madam C.J. Walker.

The 'why' has to be for you. But the next step is to know who you serve. Every business should see itself as a service organization. You need to understand the people you aim to serve, who they are, that they will not be the same as we are, and have compassion, too.

The second step is to attain a clear definition of what problem you are solving. If you define the wrong problem, you develop the wrong solution that no one needs. Durell says that in Silicon Valley, he sees this often, with founders getting millions of dollars in investment but failing because they have not followed this step. When you talk to the people you serve, you can let them tell you what problems they have.

You also need to decide if the problem is what Durell describes as a 'hair on fire' problem. He explained it to me as someone who has their hair on fire but also has an itch on their leg – two problems, but one needs solving immediately. Durell says that people are always interested in doing good, but they are compelled to stop pain. Find something that they care about deeply and a solution that is simple for 'hair on fire' needs.

The third phase is the ideation, where you start to form your ideas on how to solve it. Entrepreneurs sometimes confuse problems with solutions. If someone is not reaching their full potential, it might be that they don't consistently have food, or they may not have the education or a global pandemic could be stopping them deliver a service. Then those become the problems that need addressing. Each will have different solutions and some may not resonate with their core needs.

Many of us become too attached to an idea when we start our businesses. Durell says, by all means, hold on to it, but be ready to ditch it also. Everything in the early days is assumption based on your experience. Go on too long with this and you will start to try to change the people you are delivering to, be it the way they act or the way they do something to create a need in them that justifies your solution. You create a ladder to the answers where the rungs are just out of reach when it is your job to create a ladder people can use. No real problem means no real need for your business long term.

Then you have the prototype stage, where you are building your idea, innovation, business. Up to this point, everything you have done has been guesswork. The best thing to do is to create the smallest, simplest, fastest way to get feedback from the people you serve. Rushing in and getting investment before this is premature. Their input will highlight the bits people don't like, or might even show that they may even hate it all, but the great thing is you can learn and adapt and find out why without it affecting your overall goal. This process can be applied at every stage of your business, on each project and each new idea. And remember, your business will always be an improving prototype.

Key takeaways:

- Only by working towards your North Star will you find the energy to persevere;
- Base all plans on information from the people you plan to serve;
- Businesses that have not clarified the correct problem will ultimately fail.

5

The Importance of Values
Nicole Lamond, Eloments Tea

NICOLE'S STORY

Nicole Lamond was raised by a single mum. Growing up, the family was poor and from a young age, she was aware of injustice. Nicole learned that what happened to people was not always their fault. She grew up as a passionate believer that everyone should have equal access to education and healthcare. You can't expect people to be content when they do not have enough to eat or the means to better their own lives, as she points out. Her strongest influence was her Russian grandmother, who talked a lot about the socialist system.

Nicole did not finish high school, dropping out at 16. She took sales jobs to keep herself financially above water, while living a slightly nomadic life and pursuing her passion for skydiving, culminating in participating in the national championships. Years later, after getting married, she had three children and settled down.

During the 1990s, she spent a few months travelling throughout both India and Africa. In 1998, Nicole visited a tea plantation in Kenya, where she was fascinated by the stories of the people who worked there. She discovered that despite working full time, they couldn't afford to send their children to school or even have the most basic necessities. Appalled, Nicole started to question the ethics of how businesses could run like this and wondered how this might be changed.

She returned home and started reading about fair trade and trade justice. Fairtrade had hardly emerged in Australia, but she was compelled by its moral imperative and started investigating further. The Fairtrade system aims to ensure that workers and small farmers in developing countries get paid fairly for their work. In 1999, Nicole imported and re-sold the first Fairtrade tea into Australia from a certified co-operative. At first, she focused on selling Fairtrade tea and coffee to companies touting their ethical and corporate social responsibility credentials. Her first big sale was to The Body Shop. However, sales were slow and it was tough to pick up new customers, especially while also having full-time care of three babies and then toddlers, and revenue hovered under AU$100,000 for the first few years.

By 2002, realizing that she didn't have the skills to take the business to the next level, Nicole decided to go to university and signed up for a master's degree in business administration but found it 'somewhat boring'. In 2002, she swapped to study entrepreneurship at Swinburne University in Melbourne and immediately loved it. That same year, she became one of the founding board members of the Fairtrade Association of Australia and New Zealand and is considered one of the pioneers of Fairtrade in Australia.

In 2008, she got the Qi Teas brand into Woolworths, which has 900 stores in Australia. It became one of the store's best-selling specialist teas and was the most innovative brand on the shelves for some years until larger competitors released similar tea products. Qi Teas was a strategic choice of brand to distribute. It was manufactured at the source in China, in a remote mountain community, providing valuable employment and more impact for farmers and the local community.

In 2016, after many years of running a successful tea business, Nicole had come up with another business idea: a vitamin tea. Being healthy was very important to her and many speciality tea drinkers, and half of them purchased vitamin supplements. The problem with supplements, though, was that people bought them full of good intentions but then forgot to take them. Most people also hate taking tablets, but with 5 per cent of Australians still not eating enough fruit and vegetables, vitamin supplements have become necessary to achieve a healthy diet. Nicole's idea was simply to put the much-needed vitamins into the tea. She knew she could sell it, but had no idea how to go about manufacturing it.

Back in 2010, at a writers' group in Melbourne, she had met Julie Hirsch. For around five years, they were so immersed in the book club that they did not compare notes on work. When they did, Nicole suggested that Julie join her business. Julie went off to be a consultant instead, but after some months, she decided it wasn't for her and came back to Nicole and took her up on the offer. She joined the company in 2017.

They duly spent two years in the R & D phase. Finding a supplier for the 100 per cent natural vitamins and minerals was their first challenge. The solution was eventually found in a small family business in California called Orgenetics. With the help of an Australian dietician and nutritionist, they created a blend of vitamins and minerals.

The next challenge was finding a way to blend the vitamins into the tea in a natural way, without using synthetic binders or other manufacturing aids. Trying to do this gave them enormous manufacturing problems. The vitamins and minerals came in a powder format, which simply fell out of the tea bags. This powder needed to be changed into granules. By the end, they had an entirely innovative manufacturing process and were manufacturing in the UK. They had created the world's first natural vitamin tea. It has nine essential vitamins and minerals in every cup, no additives and was a 'clean label' product. Clean label products are as close to their natural state as possible, with only a few simple ingredients.

The time spent on R & D was long and stressful. Nicole asserts that the old saying that everything will cost twice as much and take twice as long was right, just several times over. They were cash strapped and are still very frugal to this day. Nicole says she believes business success lies in staying focused on the critical aspects of your business and not getting distracted, being robust in eliminating waste and nailing costs. She also warns against careless sales forecasting, explaining that you must work out your sales projections from the bottom up, backing them with a hard and fast plan as to exactly how you are going to attain those sales. Nicole advises all business owners that it is essential they do the grunt work, to control and crunch the numbers minutely. She says she is often telling Julie, 'Spending money doesn't mean you have a business – spending money is the easy part!'

By the end of 2018, Eloments was ready to launch and they had both retailers and consumers keen to buy. Nicole used her contacts and they struck a deal with Woolworths. Within the first 12 months, they had made deals with more than 2,000 stores in Australia and the UK, some EU countries and seen additional interest from the Middle East and Asia.

Until that year, the company had been operating on minimum finances raised from themselves, friends and families. They could not hope to continue to achieve growth without proper funding so they started looking at venture capital in Australia, but after a few meetings, Nicole says that she felt no commonality to the values of the people they met. The response was lukewarm, bar continual comments of how unusual it was to see women in the room. Nicole and Julie ended up concluding a Series A funding round for AU$1 million with a group of investors in the US who are committed to organic farming and connected with their supplier, Orgenetics. They were able to retain control and the majority shareholding. It works perfectly because their values are aligned – the investors loved the Fairtrade aspect.

There are still continual challenges. Nicole says she always worries about cash flow. Their warehouse recently gave them just two weeks' notice to move out and relocate. They still sub-contract the manufacturing and lost a big order recently because the manufacturer failed to provide the right paperwork in time. But they have gone global.

Their long-term plan is for Eloments to be the leading global vitamin tea brand, with an underlying purpose to accelerate the world's transition to a living income for all, in which Nicole believes fair trade can play a vital role. Their investors don't have a particular exit plan in mind, so everyone is open to possibilities of exit, part exit or crowdfunding in five years. Up to that point, their continued expansion is all planned.

Nicole's definition of personal success: To *'know that she has done her best, has evolved and learned in her life.'*

THE IMPORTANCE AND RELEVANCE OF VALUES

It seemed to me that Nicole was the perfect person to ask to talk of both her experiences and knowledge on the subject of company values. I could see how the values had made Eloments successful and how much they motivated her. I wanted to ask how she thought businesses without such a foundation in ethics should approach values and if they would be as important. Nicole explained it like this:

'The first major role values and ethics can play in your business is to determine your underlying purpose of why your business exists and why it's so important to you. There are elements of psychology included in this because it's about your personal motivation, so it often takes a bit of unpacking, so don't give up if it doesn't come easy. Everyone cares about something, so find out what that is.

'The second role of values is to determine what product or service you are actually producing by asking the questions "What sort of contribution do I want to make?" "How can I utilize my company's strengths to provide something that helps society?" Ideally, your product would tie into your purpose.'

Nicole points out that values led to the development of Eloments and the company and tea would not have existed without them, or had she not been so passionate about natural foods. While in the development stage of Eloments, it would have been so much easier to use synthetic or non-organic ingredients, but the commitment to organic farming kept her and her business partner Julie searching for a manufacturing process that would deliver what they wanted.

Thirdly, says Nicole, values can guide how you do business. Well-thought-out values can guide you and your staff in regards to tackling everyday difficult decisions; they are like signposts, and once embedded into the organization, drive a positive culture.

Their values are: ethics, elite (in the sense of wanting to be really good at what they do), transparency, 'New New New' (as in innovation), care of the environment (they are, of course, certified organic) and ego. I thought ego was a slightly odd one, but they define it with their office motto of 'Don't be a dick'. Nicole explains that you cannot do a good job and be a great professional with a big ego. You will not be able to open your mind to consider all the options. No one with an ego would last long around herself and Julie, she says.

In traditional corporate culture, success is about money and goals, but giving something your best effort and your best intentions as well. Nicole also believes in the wisdom of knowing what you can and can't change and accepting the latter, which you need to understand when it comes to developing business strategy.

She sees the results of having a company with such strong values all the time, particularly when it comes to developing partnerships with customers and suppliers. And, of course, their investors. Nicole and Julie believe in seeing both sides and always treating people fairly. The ability to remove yourself from the situation and think analytically, while also listening to your intuition, is one of the best skills you can develop as a business leader. She admits that when people are stressed, standing back is not always easy. Nicole says that when you value fairness more than getting your way or making an extra dollar, it becomes easier to do that, as you are not necessarily just trying to protect your own interests. People like that about the company, too. She has been fascinated by people and psychology ever since she was young and now always works to spot negativity and turn it around. To her, it is all an essential part of professional and personal development.

I asked Nicole what happens to the values as the company expands and more team members join. She told me that the core values cannot ever change. Indeed, she felt so strongly about Fairtrade being the purpose of the company that it was written into the company's constitution, so it will remain even if she is not a majority shareholder one day.

Remember, as Nicole says, 'all actions have an impact, whatever job you are doing. Everyone will leave their mark on the earth and the lives of others, so I think you may as well be purposeful about it and live a life that will be satisfying in the moment and for the long term. People are hard-wired to do meaningful work and business leaders can contribute by giving jobs, whether it's software coding, cleaning or whatever, a purpose.'

Key takeaways:

- Values give a purpose to what you do;
- They should act as a guide to what you do and how you do it;
- They can create powerful alliances with suppliers and investors who have similar values.

PART TWO

Funding

Scaling needs cash, and plenty of it. It might be for bigger premises, for more wages, for more marketing, for better systems, for both more and better people, or just more cash flow. It may well be for all of those.

As I grew, both haphazardly and ignorantly, I found myself disastrously short of cash on a couple of occasions, both involving new premises. The first time, I had to resort to borrowing a vast sum of money off the ads in the Sunday papers. The second, I used invoice finance, an option only open to B2B businesses. With invoice finance, you sell your invoices to the finance company and get paid a percentage immediately, thus alleviating your cash-flow problem. It is also costly, but worth considering for a short-term solution.

The best solution, however, is always to self-fund your growth. With the increase in other options available in the past few years, from incubators, accelerators, crowdfunding and even venture capital straying into the early-stage territory, more businesses have been able to borrow. Seasoned entrepreneurs debate the wisdom of this and whether or not the high valuations in particular are sustainable.

In this section, we look at different experiences for the main ways to fund your growth. Alex Packham shares his experiences of what it's like to go on an accelerator scheme and Ben Revell talks about how he used crowdfunding successfully. Russell Dalgleish explains the differences and relative merits of venture capitalists and Angels. David Siegel gives us an eye-opening, alternative view to the world of venture capital, while Roby Sharon-Zipser advises on how to pitch to investors.

6

Growth Via an Accelerator
Alex Packham, ContentCal

ALEX'S STORY

From an early age, Alex Packham was fascinated by the concept of money and the freedom he could see that it could bring. His parents encouraged him to earn and in his early teens, he had a job doing a paper round. Alex loathed it and quickly became convinced there were better ways to earn £15.00 a week. In those playground years, he hustled in all sorts of different ways. He progressed from selling sweets to acquiring free SIM cards, which O2 were giving away at the time, and selling them for £20.00.

At 16, he had to do work experience and he arranged to go to his uncle's film prop company. Alex learned a lot from his uncle and made up his mind that he too wanted his own business. His uncle would later become Alex's first investor and an early client.

Alex went on to study international business management at Cardiff University. He spent a lot of time on Facebook and started to notice how much influence social media feeds and friends' recommendations have on our buying patterns.

Describing himself as an early geek, Alex developed a small digital consultancy to supplement his income. He was given some wise advice and told to get some commercial experience before launching his own company. He went to work for Odeon Cinemas, running all their social marketing. From there, he took a position with a small division of Sky called NowTV, which was to be their answer to Netflix. NowTV went from 40 to 1,000 people in the two years Alex was with them so it had a real feel of a fast-growth start-up journey. They also had massive budgets, which meant great experience.

Sky allowed him to reduce his days to three a week while he was starting his own agency, ASTP, just until it got off the ground. It grew quickly to a team of nearly 20 and Alex learned the nitty-gritty of how to build teams and how to invoice people. Turnover was soon near the £1m mark, but he could see it wasn't going to give him the scale-up experience he was looking for. Agencies are not very scalable and VCs, as he was to discover, tend not to be interested in service industries. Meanwhile, he had an idea in his mind borne out of the frustration of working multi-spread sheets for each different social media and still having to assemble the information into reports at the end of studying them. That idea would become a platform called ContentCal. He became more and more convinced of the idea through talking to his agency clients that everyone, big and small, suffered from this same problem.

To start the idea, Alex conducted a fundraiser through networking with friends and family and raised £150,000, which was enough for the prototype MVP (minimal viable product) testing version. His first clients were Sky and Odeon Cinemas, so really early on, ContentCal had great client logos and monetization. It was going well, but still fell far short of Alex's ambitious plans.

In 2015, Alex applied for a place with the Accelerator Academy. Only three weeks in, his mentor, Colin Smith, told him he was going to invest. The course had told Alex they were not remotely interested in his agency, but Colin suggested they merge the agency with ContentCal.

Over the next year, Colin and Alex raised £1m and merged the two companies. Funding meant he could bring all his freelancers in-house. Three years after the course, they had raised a further £1.6m, a small team and £1m of repeating revenue. They wanted to raise another £2m for Series A funding for a growth spurt last year. Alex went back to the accelerator and asked for advice. They invited him to the next VC networking breakfast, which meant he could do an informal pitch. Within two weeks, he had a term sheet – a bullet-point letter of intent setting out the terms and conditions of the agreement.

Alex says he owes the accelerator a huge amount. Not only is he growing ContentCal all the time now, but he is also on the board of a couple of other companies. To his pleasure, this includes his uncle's company, Prop Store, along with Kindred, a business Alex co-founded with a friend, after these too started to grow fast. Now it is Alex's turn to hand out advice and give back to the person who inspired and helped him at the start.

Alex's definition of personal success: *'Having freedom. Building and selling business means being able to do whatever I like, including perhaps having a month or two off. It means not being beholden to others and having them tell you what you can and can't do. Also, entrepreneurs are seen as this slightly different breed. So while we do, of course, have imposter syndrome, along the way, you gradually realize it is OK to be yourself.'*

GROWTH VIA AN ACCELERATOR

Accelerators are appearing in fast-growing numbers round the globe. Perhaps the most famous of all are Tech Stars and the prestigious Y Combinator. I asked Alex to share more of his experience of his course and his thoughts on how other people should go about choosing an accelerator for their journey. He told me that he had recently been talking to NESTA, who had been researching accelerators. There is no expert service to monitor or steer choices and there are now more than 100 accelerators in a myriad of sectors, with more forming all the time, which makes it a big challenge to choose the right one.

I was interested in finding out how Alex had managed such a successful choice. He told me that he had started asking around on Twitter. He had also gone to an accelerator networking event but found it fairly poor. In the end, he heard of the right one via a personal recommendation. He chose based on his talks with people involved, finding he related to what was being said, and his gut instinct.

The Accelerator Academy that Alex attended offers a 12-week high-growth programme for digital entrepreneurs. In common with other accelerators, it delivers a mix of training, mentoring and access to capital. Alex told me it was a very strict process to get in and the level expected from applicants was high. He was to discover that most of the other candidates were initial start-ups and it was unusual for someone like himself, with two years' trading, to be on the course.

The cost was £600 and a relatively small piece of equity in the company each for both the course organizers and the allocated mentor. One thing that impressed Alex was that this particular course only had mentors who could show that they had actively invested within the last year rather than large numbers of inactive networkers.

Alex told me that on the first day, he very nearly didn't go as he was ill and feeling atrocious. He staggered in and sat at the back, noting everything down. They had lectures every Monday afternoon and homework during the rest of the week, which he juggled with running his agency. It was made easier by the course being well structured, with one week per subject. Alex describes it as a mini start-up MBA, covering all the fundamentals of how to scale up. At the end, you have a ready-made plan to pitch to 100 investors in a formal setting. One of the benefits of this is that it gets your name out there into the VC community, as everyone you want to know about you is in that room.

Alex strongly advises people to take at least a month or two to explore the options and to talk to those involved in any accelerator programme, as well as those who have been on the course. Many will have failed, as did most on Alex's course, but you can check and assess the reasons. Selection is all a case of doing careful due diligence. Alex also believes that however good the course, in the end it is up to your attitude what you achieve with it.

For Alex, the value has been far more than just the course itself. The people there have remained in his life. It was to them he turned for advice when he wanted to do a Series A funding round. He met his mentor and now chairman through them, as well as many of his investors. The course has provided him with an all-round support system.

> **Key takeaways:**
>
> - Connect with the people running the course and get to know them;
> - Look at the companies who have been through the course before;
> - Carefully consider the deal offered, especially regarding the amount of equity needed.

7

Crowdfunding to Disrupt the World of Wine

Ben Revell, Winebuyers.com

Ben Revell is another excellent example of a disruptive entrepreneur, someone who has taken an existing business model and turned it upside down. Winebuyers is his fourth company in the luxury goods market. I asked Ben where the passion for starting businesses originated. He says being an entrepreneur wasn't so much a conscious decision as something he just fell into by chance: 'As a child, I was obsessed with building things. If I went to a city and saw people carving little sculptures out of wood, I was convinced that I could do it, so I'd go back home and do exactly that. So, I've gone from building things to trying to build businesses.'

Ben had his first lightbulb moment when he was about 12. His parents used to give him pocket money for doing chores around the house and he remembers one weekend getting £10 for mowing the lawn on a Saturday. He paid his friend

Matthew down the road to do it for £5.50. That was his eureka moment. Coupled with a desire to get into every area that he can, this approach makes a good fit for an entrepreneur.

The wine came slightly later. At 18, and studying at university, Ben visited an auction house and made a hugely ambitious bid for Lot 219, a case of 1959 Bordeaux, Château Margaux. The figure was around half the book valuation and he was amazed to win. He sold the case just three days later for £6,200, a very tidy little profit of £2,500. Not surprisingly, Ben decided this was worth pursuing and within three months had built up a stock of 500 bottles to sell. By 2013, he had formed Prestigious Wine Ltd.

He continued to trade in wine as a side business, but it wasn't until 2015 that he realized there was a gap in the market and started planning Winebuyers. Using £3,700 from his savings, he worked with a website team to build the bespoke technology that is at the heart of Winebuyers. Explaining how significant the potential is, Ben told me, 'Wine is no longer just for the connoisseur. The UK has over 30 million regular wine consumers across all regions, ages and social classes, with 77 per cent of UK adults buying goods or services online in the last 12 months. The future of the wine market is online and smaller wineries and merchants are looking to e-commerce to maximize their margins.'

Winebuyers is radically different from its competitors. Ben explains, 'The concept is completely new to the industry, in giving smaller vineyards the chance to reach consumer audiences they otherwise could not, encouraging growth by maximizing their margins. Our aim is simple: we're using technology to bring the wine industry into the twenty-first century. We cut out the middleman and connect wine lovers directly to the best vineyards and merchants in the world. We want to offer something exciting and provide variety to the consumer. Rather than charge the consumer, it is the producers who pay a small monthly subscription instead.'

I am always fascinated by how people spot the gap. Ben told me, 'While I set up the company to satisfy my interest in investing in fine wines and champagnes, you could say the project was borne out of necessity. There wasn't any viable way to sell these types of products online. At that time, you were not able to sell on Amazon and to this day, you can't sell them on eBay UK; auctions charge 20 per cent commission. I identified a gap in the market, which led me to establish Winebuyers.'

There are no hidden fees and members can cancel their free subscription at any time. Also, consumers benefit from special offers and recommendations from wine specialists on the site. But the major business differential is that this advice is entirely impartial because Winebuyers has nothing to gain from selling one wine over another. This trust and transparency has also been key to their success.

Ben says that in the short term they want to keep on improving the technology behind their smart platform, develop new features and grow their team. 'We've got a really good team at the moment,' he told me, 'especially our web developers, who are amazing. They blow me away. Getting the right people on board is the most important thing. We've got quite a wide team with varied backgrounds from luxury goods to the wine industry. Ciara, our head of marketing, who comes from an events background, is brilliant. We've also taken on board some apprentices who are fantastic and so enthusiastic about the product. It's nice to have a team that fully supports the idea of connecting the vineyard directly to the consumer.'

His vision is for Winebuyers to lead the forefront of the e-commerce wine business. Winebuyers is now valued at £10m on today's markets, and has a five-year exit plan. It all sounds easy, but of course, it hasn't been. Ben warns that to build a successful business, 'You have to sacrifice – you have to be willing to work really hard. Being your own boss looks great, but you have to be willing to put in the work and a lot of hours.'

Ben's original £3,700 was merely a tiny start. The company has needed large-scale funding. Of more than £1m raised, over half came from crowdfunding. He used an equity investment platform called Crowdcube.

'Everyone can have ideas,' says Ben, 'but without funds, you won't go anywhere. Getting an idea is one thing, but you need to understand the pragmatic side of the business. That is key.'

Ben's definition of personal success: *'Success to me is freedom, whatever form that takes, be it financial or otherwise. The ability to do what you desire and the means to make it happen. Resilience is key; you have to be willing to work harder and longer than everybody else to succeed. You need to be 100 per cent committed to doing whatever it takes to execute your vision. I think being an entrepreneur is often perceived as a glamorous endeavour. However, the reality is it is anything but, it is all-encompassing and all-consuming, you need to devote everything you have to the cause in order to succeed. I believe the phrase "Learn* *from your mistakes" is terribly misguided. Why not "Learn from other people's mistakes"? We live in a connected world, assimilate information from all sources and build a support network/team to guide you on your way. Monetary wealth is often just a by-product of achievement – achieve your goals one step at a time and the rest will follow.'*

CROWDFUNDING

Several entrepreneurs in this book, including Ben, have chosen the crowdfunding route to raise capital for their businesses. Crowdfunding is well known for raising money for charity, but this online platform is making it an increasingly attractive option for businesses.

There are three main types. The reward type will offer something in return for the investment, where the investor gets something the company sells at a discount or for free. There is credit-based crowdfunding, where individual investors can be put in touch with a company wanting to borrow money. Finally, there is equity-based crowdfunding, such as Ben used, where investors buy shares in unlisted companies.

Crowdfunding websites introduce investors to companies looking for investment. Loans are often not available to new business people and many business owners are not comfortable with taking on large-size debt, which means that crowdfunding can be an attractive proposition.

A side benefit to crowdfunding is that it gives the new company exposure to people with both interest and knowledge in the industry. Ben says, 'One of the things that came off the back of crowdfunding, which I didn't anticipate, was the fact that we had 300 people invest, a lot of them in the industry. They've got such a wealth of knowledge behind them. It's great to get their opinions and strategies. It's nice to be able to utilize the skills of people who have a vested interest in the company succeeding. You get invaluable feedback and market testing pre-launch.'

Take time and care, choosing the crowdfunding platform that is right for you. Choosing the wrong one could have a very negative effect on your brand's image. Be realistic about the amount of money you seek. It tends to be easier for consumer products as people can see and understand what they are investing in. Success relies on a good idea and a business plan with robust financial forecasts.

Creating a video will help you gain traction in the market and can get you great publicity as well. Ensure that in addition to showing why your business is going to work, you and your story shine too. Often, it is an emotional connection that tips people into investing.

Crowdfunding is a very cost-effective way of raising cash for your business, but be aware of the downsides. You need to be sure of the actual plan because the investors, reasonably, will expect you to follow it. Another huge danger is that you are putting your idea out into the public domain. It is, therefore, essential that you consult an intellectual property expert and take every step to protect against IP theft before you take that plunge.

I asked Ben to talk me through his experiences with fundraising: 'Funding is the most difficult thing at the moment. We're at a time where banks aren't forthcoming in lending, so it can be difficult to raise finance, let alone if you're 18 or 19, walking into a bank with a business plan asking for money. I can't tell you how many people said no to me; it was probably upwards of 100. That's why we decided to go down the crowdfunding route.

'The crowdfunding campaign on Crowdcube lasted 30 days, but in reality, the work behind the lead-up to it is probably one year to 14 months. You have to be so well prepared, from your business plans to everything else. On the front end, it could look like you put up a video and watch the money roll in, but it couldn't be further from the truth.

'For crowdfunding, preparation is critical. You need the ability to have prepared answers for all interested parties. It's a very public way of getting to proof of concept. If you go on a public forum like this and it doesn't go well, then it could cause you problems. It's hard work. It looks super easy, but it's certainly not. Preparation and having a good campaign in the run-up to it, and trying to get an initial injection of capital before you even go live, will significantly help.

'With a regulated platform like Crowdcube, you've done a great job to even get on there. There are a lot of legal hoops that you need to jump through to get yourself listed. Don't go on Crowdcube prematurely. You could just put up a video and hope for the best, but it's a long, hard slog. It's all in the planning.

'With Crowdcube, it's an all-or-nothing situation. You have to achieve your target or you don't get a penny. Investments come in very sporadically. There are lots of people asking questions and you have to answer them comprehensively enough to convince them to commit their money to you. It's a big ask and we're very thankful that it all went smoothly in the end.'

Key takeaways:

- Research and choose the right platform with care;
- Crowdfunding success comes from the preparation – expect to take one to two years;
- A side benefit is that people who invest often bring specialist market knowledge.

8

Angels and VCs and How to Prepare

Russell Dalgleish, Exolta Capital Partners

Russell Dalgleish was born in Selkirk, on the Scottish borders. His family had lived there for 400 years. Russell was the first person in the family to reach further education. He chose to study technology at Edinburgh's Napier University, a decision he says was based on having just seen *Star Wars*. He recalls that he struggled, only 'just' graduating. From there, Russell took a position with the Bank of Scotland. After four-and-a-half years, they sat him down and told him he could either be a banker or a developer, but not both. He went home, thought about it, decided he wanted to be neither and resigned the next day.

Russell did, however, want to stay within technology, so he went to work for an electronics company in Fife that made credit card terminals. He says he learned a vast amount there. His next move was to Calluna, which made the three-and-a-half-inch floppy discs for computers. These were first copywritten in Scotland. He was the only non-engineer, hired to take all the incoming calls that were sidetracking the real engineers. On his first day, he got a call from a Russian sub in the morning. Then, in the afternoon, he was talking to NASA. Russell stayed there for more than four years, adding cross-sector value. He was travelling continually, juggling the calls from NASA, the long-haul flights and taking his young family to nursery school. One day, his flight from Heathrow to Tokyo was diverted to Frankfurt. The air hostess came and asked him if he was OK. Russell said he was fine and asked her why. She pointed out gently that he was crying – demands in all directions had stretched him too thin and everything had caught up with him.

Russell decided to start over and took a job as a salesman for a software company. A second, similar position followed, where he helped to build the company and ended up as MD. It was the start of his career in scaling tech companies. A spell in the mid-1990s also saw him establish a business in San Jose, California, where he says, 'Silicon Valley really was still Silicon.' This experience had a profound effect on him, seeing for himself how two guys working in a garage could become millionaires overnight. It taught him that there are no limits.

Russell has a low tolerance for people who do not use the phenomenal opportunities offered by the Internet, of being able to find out about, for example, the competition by merely leaping on to Google. He says that much of his success is owed to him being a geek.

At the end of the 1990s, he became involved in doing turnarounds, rescuing businesses from near failure. The first, with which he has retained close business ties ever since, took him to London. I asked if it was these experiences that prompted him to discuss the value of talking to the people in the canteen, on the shop floor. Russell points out that if you ask the people on the board, they will only tell you all the things that got them into trouble in the first place, whereas connecting at all levels of a business is a classic turnaround technique.

Russell then tells me how he went to one London company, which also had just three people in Sheffield. He asked what one of them did and was told, 'You don't have to worry about her, she just runs the help desk.' When Russell met her, he discovered that she was the only person in the company who dealt with the customers.

Russell also believes that process is the key to success. He explains that, if there is just one of you, you know everything that is going on. With two of you, you have to be careful and ensure you share all the information. By the time you are 20, it is incredibly hard to stay abreast of everything, and by the time you have 100 people involved, you have to optimize it. You can only do that by studying and documenting processes. You need a skeleton framework to attach the best people for the right job and support them to win.

Russell says he doesn't have much self-doubt and, indeed, tends to have more than his share of confidence. Failure, he says, doesn't fuss him. He has 'done some things that have gone terribly wrong and some that have gone terribly right.' But he says that he has been helped by having both resilience and emotional intelligence.

Leadership is something he speaks of regularly. Russell believes that leadership lies in knowing who you are. A lot of the time, he says, we lie to ourselves and looking accurately in a mirror can be a shock. He uses himself as an example and says he has come to know that he likes being loved, being on stage and travelling. While it was opportunistic rather than deliberately strategic, he has ended up speaking all over the world.

He is a great believer in being opportunistic. In the course of our conversation, I told him that my father was from Aberdeen, a city Russell believes has produced some of the greatest Scottish entrepreneurs. He tells me the story of Ian Wood, who joined the modest family firm in the North Sea oil industry. One day, an American came to see him in his office, complete with Stetson and cowboy boots. At the end of the meeting, Ian offered to call him a taxi.

'I have one outside,' came the response. Stunned by such extravagance, Ian exclaimed, 'You haven't had him wait all this time?' The American replied easily, 'No, I have had him for the whole week.' Sir Ian Wood, as he later became, saw the size of the opportunity in such unheard-of extravagance and quickly flew out to Houston for their next meeting. From there, he was largely responsible for turning the firm into a massive corporation with operations in more than 50 countries.

We divert briefly to talk about Russell's latest passion for endurance events, which he says also came from being opportunistic. When he was 49, someone asked him to take part in one of these events. He decided that he would treat it as a challenge to become fitter than he had ever been in his life. Russell approached the task as he would a business. He started with a plan, learned a lot, went through repetitious actions, got a coach, formed a team and even raised capital to buy the best possible equipment.

Meanwhile, his current day job is running Exolta Capital, which offers advisory services, including helping companies obtain funding. Russell is also an Angel Investor through the private equity firm Par Equity. He is on the board of 10 companies, including IoD Scotland and the Scottish Board of Trade.

Russell observes that often we mistakenly believe that people will know what we do, or recognize the problem our business solves. But they don't and the solution is to get out there and talk. Through his work with the IoD, he saw that Scots companies were just not getting their message out there enough. In 2016, Russell set up the Scottish Business Network with Christine Esson to solve this. They started with a centre in London. The SBN now has 8,000 members globally and aims for a network in every city of the world. They provide advice, sales support and desk space to members, as well as holding regular networking events.

Russell is listed as one of the top 100 most influential British entrepreneurs and one of the top three in technology. He divides his time between his London-based interests and his home in Linlithgow, some 65km (40 miles) from Edinburgh. When I ask him what the future holds, he says it is a time of tremendous opportunities and he is 'just going to keep doing what I'm doing'.

He is a man who lives in the moment.

Russell's personal definition of success: *'To build our Scottish Business Network into the largest global Scottish community on Planet Earth.'*

VENTURE CAPITALISTS AND ANGEL INVESTORS

This world can be full of pitfalls for the experienced business person, let alone a novice. I have heard many stories of bad experiences raising venture capital in the course of my research. But there are success stories, too. Many businesses need to turn to these sources of investment and do so with excellent outcomes. Some achieve it via peer-to-peer lending websites, some through personal contacts and others through firms such as Exolta for advice on funding.

With VC funding, the firm you choose will in part depend on whether or not you are looking for early or later-stage funding. Early stage funding will be formal in structure and requires larger equity to make up for high risk, but may well include some super-Angels behind the deal who will stay with you through the journey and later growth. Other companies are only interested in funding later-stage deals.

One of the chief differentials between Angel Investors and VCs or indeed VCTs (venture capital trusts) is that Angels use their own money to invest, while VCs use other people's. Their money comes from individuals, corporations and pension funds. It is a vital difference that influences everything about the deal and the approach.

Traditionally, VCs invested in expanding companies but are now getting involved in investing in start-ups. Individual VCs tend to look at companies in earlier development and VCTs at more mature companies. They mainly put in amounts of £1m-plus to get a proportionate return on their work and investment. Typically, they look for 25–35 per cent and a healthy return on their investment, and at least 50 per cent growth.

Business Angels are often former business people themselves, or those interested in investing money directly into private companies. Some work alone, others in groups. Under the Financial Conduct Authority in the UK, investors have to do a self-certification to show that they are of high net worth. Amounts tend to range between £10,000 and £500,000, though groups can go up to £2m. Both will want equity in your business. Angels also look for good profits and their risks are even higher as in the early stages, profitability tends to be unproven. VCs will want to terminate the investment at some point and will sometimes sell shares back to the owner, but mainly sell the shares through a public offering, or sell the whole company. While some will help develop the business, the focus tends to be on exit strategies. Angels will tend to be more focused on building a business and also offer advice and contacts.

Few VCs mentor, whereas many Angels will. Both will have access to contacts, and advisors and VCs in particular tend to have excellent connections for senior talent. Some Angels invest to give back as well as to make returns. Angels vary in how much they wish to be hands-on or hands-off, and how much advice and mentoring they are offering. They will, understandably, have some say in what you do and some may want a seat on the board.

VCs invariably want a seat on the board. They will structure the deal to enable themselves to get their way in decisions. Their involvement does, however, help focus on goals. Business owners have to come to terms with moving from being in control to being an employee, and with having become a commodity. Both Angels and VCs will require regular detailed reporting.

A deal with a VC takes time. They will do in-depth research and apply due diligence. Borrowers can be in a Catch-22 situation where they don't know much about any deal they might be offered until it is complete. At that point, there can be some heavy pressure to go ahead because the VCs will not want to lose the money they have already spent and the owners will often be desperate for capital by then.

Angel Investors tend to be easier to convince in pitches and have much shorter decision times as they are free to make their own decisions if they work alone. They draw on their personal experience to judge business ideas before commercial results, focusing much more on the individual, the offering, the market and why the business has the potential to succeed, rather than current figures.

Raising finance is a huge undertaking. It is wise to test how much you need it by laying out what your plans for the next few years could look like, with and without the investment, and good and bad outcomes. Doing this will help you focus on risk and return. You also need to be very sure if you are looking to exit and that you and the investors are on the same page on this. And of course, take extensive legal advice.

Research the possible investor. Talk to other people they have invested in, those who have and haven't survived. Talk to independent financial advisors. Assess if the investor fully understands both what you do and your market. Remember, there are sharks out there. For investors, you are a money-making commodity. There is no room for them to play nice.

Both as an Angel and as a VC, Russell looks for two things only: the market opportunity and the team. He says that if someone starts talking to him about their product, he stops them – he is not interested.

Key takeaways:

- Be alert to, and ready to grab all opportunities;
- There is no such thing as too much research when it comes to investment;
- Be aware VCs will want to exit at some point regardless of whether you do.

9

Inside Venture Capital

David Siegel, Venture Partner, Right Side Capital Management

David Siegel spent his childhood splitting his time between Salt Lake City and Denver after his parents divorced. His lifetime habit of putting moon-shot ideas out there to see which stuck started early on. At 15, David wrote to Adolf 'Adi' Dassler, founder of Adidas, putting forward a concept for a boot for fly fishers. Dassler replied, saying that it was a ridiculous idea, but he could choose a free pair of Adidas. David believes the 'things that don't bounce, have chosen him', his own version of trusting things to fate.

David says he wasn't a great student, so when he applied to Stanford, Cornell and Wichita, he couldn't get in. Instead, he studied applied mathematics at the University of Colorado Boulder. Still determined to get into Stanford, David tried five times. He makes the case that the more shots you take, the more likely you are to succeed.

David managed to get on to Don Kruth's typeface programme. Kruth was one of the top computer scientists in the world and David became one of the first people to work on computer programs that created typefaces. He worked on TeX Metafont, a typesetting language for how you typeset equations. TeX is still used all over the world.

David always had other things on the go. When there was an industry conference at Stanford, he would be the person printing T-shirts and selling them. He helped people to write essays for their university applications to institutions such as Harvard. In return, one of them helped David get a job as a documentation writer at Pixar, which was full of amazingly smart people.

David started a company painting Macintosh computers. He would take them apart all over his living room and send the cases out for painting, before putting them back together again, ignorant of the dangers from the cathode ray tubes. He then did a deal with Apple to get empty plastic shells, pre-paint them and send them on to a dealer to swap over. John Sculley, then CEO of Apple, asked him to make a marbleized one for Malcolm Forbes as a present for his boat, the only marble Mac in the world.

David then went back to type, to make a typeface based on architects' hand lettering. Fonts still came in separate boxes then. He contacted the expert in that field, Frank Ching, paid him $5,000 to do the lettering and launched it as Tekton. It made millions and eventually, Adobe bought Tekton outright from him. David then created the Graphite typeface, which Hewlett-Packard sent out with every inkjet printer.

David also developed a technology to make contextual joined writing. He negotiated a licence to reproduce the handwriting of Andy Warhol; he also had fonts based on the handwriting of Ben Franklin, Marilyn Monroe and Jimi Hendrix. However, the processors at that point were not fast enough to use it and fonts had suddenly become dirt cheap. David says it was a case of 'Will the last typeface designer switch out the lights on their way out'.

David's next company was Verso, one of the first-ever web strategy businesses, to create and teach website design. When he sold Verso in 2000, he was a wealthy man. He had also started writing books and *Creating Killer Websites: Art of Third-generation Site Design* was in the top 10 on Amazon, and he was also doing consulting work for organizations from Amazon, the United Nations and NASA's mission to Mars.

At 40, he started Angel Investing. David says he was utterly clueless, 'investing really badly'. For 10 years, he made significant losses, putting most of it into just three companies and trying to give entrepreneurs what they needed rather than what was wise. When the biggest one collapsed, he realized it was time to change. Part of that was studying statistics and rationality.

Since then, ventures have included the Pillar Project, aiming to build the world's most advanced blockchain wallet; 20/30, a venture studio in London; and Permissionless Finance, advising start-ups to Fortune 500 companies. Another project, the Giordano Bruno Institute, aims to address broken systems, including healthcare, education and centralized finance. David continues to write books and articles on Medium.com. He is also a venture partner in Right Side Capital Management.

David's definition of personal success: *'I have had a lot, and I have had a little, and somewhere in between is a lot better than either. So now, I want a reasonable income and intellectual interest. Like most people, I simply want not to work for an asshole, have a reasonable amount of money and some meaningful work I enjoy. It isn't about being a billionaire.'*

INSIDE VENTURE CAPITALISM

David warns that his advice is not what you want to hear but what you need to hear. Venture capital investment is full of myths and entrepreneurs who turn investors mostly get out after five years. They believe they can beat the markets, but in reality, VC funds do not generally out-perform the public market. To offset risk, a VC needs to achieve 2.5x to break even over 10 years, but the average return is 1.9x.

David talks of the following fallacies of venture capital:

1 The Cause and Effect Fallacy: Both entrepreneurs and investors believe that success is down to their skill rather than luck and circumstance. They think they can make plans become realities when the reality is that you cannot predict three years ahead. For every Elon Musk, there are 1,000 people trying to get into that sunshine. Too many people fail for it to be all skill.

2 The Skill versus Luck Fallacy: The wise investor, such as Warren Buffet, says he has no idea and plays a long game with a sophisticated model to allocate capital. Hedge funds tell stories of their success but fail to show the comparison to the SNP 500 for the same period, which will almost certainly have done better. Investors have a belief that they can 'pick winners'. They listen to stories and make snap judgements, ignoring anyone else's opinion, they put less weight in data and ignore the bigger picture. David says the top 10 per cent help companies to grow, but this is more down to the sales they introduce.

3 The Fallacy that Big Numbers Behave like Small Numbers: Smart investors accept that 70 per cent of the companies they invest in will go bust. These figures mean that if you invest in 50 companies over 10 years, you have a 60 per cent chance of making 1x returns, but if you invest in 300, that percentage goes up to 99. Five hundred gets a better result still. It is a different mathematical foundation for returns. Wise investors recognize that cherry picking is a dangerous game and opt for a quantitative, data-rich approach, where yields can be 3x and more and do beat the SNP.

4 The Track Record Fallacy: In choosing an investment company, we look at their results over the last 10 years. During 10 years, a third tend to perform exceptionally well, a third poorly and the rest in between. We select the ones that are doing well, but the law of averages will mean that this third will move into one of the other groups next.

5 The Herd Mentality Fallacy: If you ask a VC for, say, half the money at the start of fundraising, you will probably get a no. Tell them you have already raised three-quarters and they will instantly want in on the deal. This factor alone is proven to be several times over more important than anything else in investment decisions.

6 Predestination Fallacy: There is a belief that some companies are predestined to do well. When investors see the progress of their 8 per cent investment and another funding round comes along, they reinvest to keep at 8 per cent. They forget that at every single stage, failure is just around the corner and now the valuation is way overpriced.

I asked David what entrepreneurs can do about this to even the odds of success and if and how they should deal with venture capitalists. He says the first thing is not to get money from people you don't know; in fairness, many are nice guys, but deluded. VCs even have their own language. They will go 'I love the look of this deal' and then not take your calls. They are polite, so they will rarely tell you 'no' straight out. They aren't that good at 'yes' either, of course, until they hear others saying it. When they look you in the eye and say keep in touch, you should know it is goodbye forever.

VCs say that all their deals come from people they know. The reality is that they have people out there doing introductions, who have already made 60–70 per cent of the decision before that introduction. So when you think it is all about your brilliant presentation, it is really about relationships instead.

David says what entrepreneurs should be doing is concentrating all their efforts on the revenue. Success is all about sales. Entrepreneurs also fall into the trap of thinking it is their skill when, in reality, those who survive have good luck and sell well.

People have become obsessed with products, and products need luck. David points out that Bill Gates didn't have a product. Instead, get your competitor's product and learn to make sales, then you can figure out a way to make yours a bit different. People raise eye-watering sums of money and then spend far too much time engineering when they could be selling. Instead of scaling too soon, take small, positive steps rather than aiming too high. Learn about the market and your customers instead.

David recommends wherever possible using pretotyping, a methodology named by Alberto Savoia at Google.

Pretotyping is selling something pre-building and learning from the research and feedback to build something far better.

Products are vulnerable to both luck and timing. David cites a company he consulted on many years back. It had tons of money poured in, a lot of exceptional guys from Google, and a brilliant teleconference product. But despite all that, Zoom managed to push it out of the market. Zoom was a product that barely worked when it started, but it didn't need any hardware, which the market preferred. So Zoom made the sale despite having a less impressive product. Zoom have also been quick to see the opportunities of Covid-19, with the majority of companies becoming reliant on their virtual meetings and conferences in the early days of the pandemic.

People get excited about new products, but the reality is that products are all very alike. VCs see similar successful products and overlook the failures because failure is the Black Web of entrepreneurship, something we don't talk about much. The markets select successful products randomly for impossible-to-predict reasons. So you need to sell, but you also need to pivot quickly.

People need to move on from the macro-economy. Instead of raising vast sums of money, you can get a no-code app built on something like Builder.ai over a weekend. You will then have a product to go out and sell.

I asked David about accelerators. He believes that except for Techstars, the accelerator and incubator models typically get no better results. They are worth joining if you can't get funding outside, but their most significant value is that they signal to the investors that a company is worth investing in: 'Unaccelerated companies who get the same amount of money do just as well,' he says.

The value-added concept is another myth. Investors will tell you how punchy they are, how they have looked at 1,000 companies before you, how much value they are going to add by turning up for board meetings and spending lots of time on the phone to you. It does not add anything. People choose advisors who tell them what they want to hear at that point to strengthen their own beliefs and when things change, they will get different ones. Gates, Zuckerberg, Jobs all got advice as they grew. VCs' opinions will not cause your growth. Instead, the right advisors turn up because you are growing. Venture capitalists do not add value and never have but simply suck cash. They make the same mistakes as everyone else.

Key takeaways:

- Recognize the hands of luck and market over skill;
- Don't obsess about product, obsess about sales;
- Few VCs add to your growth. They are playing a numbers game to take out profits.

10

How to Pitch for Funding

Roby Sharon-Zipser, hipages Group

ROBY'S STORY

Roby Sharon-Zipser's parents and grandparents both had their own businesses. As young as five, Roby was working in his grandparents' clothing business, organizing shirts on to hangers for five bucks a day. He helped his aunties in the office, cleaning, taking the rubbish out and counting inventory, alongside other odd jobs.

Roby was expected to earn and was never given pocket money. He was always doing something to make money. As a teenager, he had a car washing business. His parents' company was in retail and wholesale. For them, he sold bedlinen and carried customers' parcels to their cars on weekends and during school holidays. He also helped out with the accounting, preparing invoices, and would check and enter them into the ledger. Always strong at maths and business studies, he came out of high school good with numbers, confident in his commercial abilities.

Roby went to the University of New South Wales and was surprised to find he struggled for the first semester, but he hadn't anticipated the big difference from school, that everyone comes in at the same level. He adjusted and was out in front by the end. While at university, he had a market stall selling menswear. He ran it like a small business. Roby found some of the local kids to help. He got to keep the profit when there was some and around Christmas, he would make enough for a holiday. Unfortunately, when it rained, he didn't make any money. It was hard work standing on his feet all day, and involved early starts to set up the stall and late finishes, packing up and a long drive home.

He went to work for Price Waterhouse, later Pricewaterhouse-Coopers (PwC). Roby never saw himself as a partner – he was always working towards having his own business. In a practice, you get stuck in a specific area, in Roby's case, auditing for industry and products. He wanted a broader knowledge, particularly in tax and company structure, so he went to work for an investment bank. He also started a recovery business with a partner, but they quickly found it wasn't scalable, so they wrapped it up.

Instead, he and his childhood friend, David Vitek, started an online directory for natural therapies, an interest of David's. Natural Therapy Pages featured health, nutrition, naturopathy articles and listings of relevant facilities and practitioners. It was an extremely lean start-up, working out of a garage, and they had to keep themselves going on credit cards. Having no money meant their only option was to find customers, so they did.

Three months in, hipages came into being. They had quickly realized there was a more significant gap in the online directory market in the home improvement arena. Their bigger competitors were targeting the big companies, but no one was servicing the smaller guys. By contrast, hipages offered a comprehensive product in a market that was just coming to life. They quite literally introduced the small companies to the Internet, provided small trade businesses with the opportunity to get online and charged only a small annual fee of AU$89. They developed a strong competency in SEO (search engine optimization) and online marketing, all new at that time, and have retained this strength on an ongoing basis. They still remember the days of the 1 cent click ad.

They would say to their customers, 'If you can take a picture of your work at the end of each day, we will find the time to load it to your profile.' It was a crazy offer that a big corporation couldn't have made, which meant them working 80-hour weeks, but it worked. By year three, they had a team of 30.

They were doing things incredibly well and they were also doing them cheaper and better. To this day, one of their secrets is their low-cost structure, partly down to being incredibly lean in the way they operate and looking at international distribution models to support the needs of the people and the business. It gave them more than a decade of traction.

They had been into one round of Angel Investment, which allowed them to improve their software development and do a big sales push. By 2013, hipages were generating more than a million visitors a year, with 40,000 tradespeople listed on the directory. They had also partnered with IKEA to provide their consumers with local tradespeople who would install IKEA's kitchens.

Now, they decided to do something much bigger and pivot the business entirely. The idea was to provide a better way to connect to trades and change from being an online directory to an online marketplace where people could get quotes for the improvement or repair work they wanted. They planned, Roby explains, to beat the old ways of looking for a tradesperson by calling round and seeing who would answer your call, but rather you telling the platform what you want and trades connecting to you that are trusted and local. He refers to it as the creation of the 'On-Demand Tradie Economy'.

Money has always been the biggest challenge. In their early years, it was tough to get investment as a tech company in Australia. It has changed now, but tech was embryonic then, with most investors choosing to go into mining companies. They raised more than AU$ 6m to fund their growth from a group of investors, including Ellerston Capital. This capital meant they could invest in more technology and product development and into the brand. In 2015, News Corp Australia came to them with an offer to buy a 25 per cent stake, enabling them to grow even further.

Roby says that another of the challenges of being cash-strapped in the early years is you don't have a great environment to attract great people. You need to invest in culture and that takes time. One of his many pieces of advice is to always invest in the best possible people you can afford at any given time.

He describes it all as 'a roller coaster ride' and says that you need an outstanding leadership team where everyone is both smarter than you and better than you in their specialist areas. The bigger you get, the tougher it becomes. You have to be very resilient because there are lots of people investing in you and counting on you. It can look very appealing to go and get a well-paid job and not have all the extra baggage – you need to believe in your vision, strategy, purpose, and use all that when working with people.

hipages has continued to grow by more than 26 per cent every year. There have been some downs, inevitably, but they are the largest trade network in Australia and have more than 3 million users on the homeowner side. Their traction has enabled them to reinvest continually.

When you start to scale, Roby says, it gets tougher each leap – the 1–100, 100–200 and above that again. Each time, they continue to reinvest, because every time you scale, you need to check that the processes, costs, people and products are in place to support that growth.

hipages is now the largest company in the 'On-demand Tradie Economy'. At the end of 2020, Roby brought home a $318m ASX float.

Roby's definition of personal success: *'Building a business that has a good purpose, quality people, one that delivers an excellent value proposition to the customer.'*

HOW TO RAISE FINANCE

Roby was kind enough to share some golden advice on how to start raising finance, based on his many experiences of doing so over the years. He began by clarifying that what he talks about here is not your friends and family starter finance, but Series A, formal investment, aimed at optimizing the opportunities you have created.

Roby says the choice of first investor is always the most important as they set the scene for all those who follow. You need to find someone you like and who is in alignment with you, your business and your vision. These first investors will need to support you and talk to you, through what can otherwise be a lonely stretch of the journey. You will not have achieved a strong leadership team to help with that at this point, so your investor will play more of a partner role.

Roby says that any investor at this stage needs to be in it for the long term. Many investors now expect to pull their money out in five to seven years, whereas, in reality, they need to be in it for 10 to 15 years. He points out that all businesses have their ups and downs and side to sides too – there is never a perfect 45-degree angle to growth.

Raising money is very complex, so your first step should be to consult a high-quality, experienced and independent advisor well ahead of time. These advisors take payment in the form of a percentage of the money you raise. Part of their job is to prepare you to pitch right, challenge your assumptions and ensure you know what to expect. You will also benefit from their expertise in the complexities you face in constructing the deal itself.

When you have found your advisor and an investor you are comfortable with, then comes the time for you to pitch. You need an elevator pitch, a teaser and a pitch deck. That elevator pitch is a sentence that expresses who you are and what you do. Roby's is 'hipages is the RealEstate.com.au for home improvements'. It has to give someone off the street an instant understanding of what it is you do without them thinking too hard.

A teaser is different. It is a one-page summary of all the highlights of the business opportunity that you are proposing. Its purpose is to get the investors even more interested in you. It does not include financial projections or sales pitches.

A pitch deck is a presentation that you put together when seeking investment to give potential investors a brief overview. It should be around 10 slides in total. These should include one each showing what problem you are solving, your product and technical sides, the market size and the opportunity and the traction, your financial metrics and then, of course, the ask.

Once you have presented, then come the questions. You need to know your numbers and you must be crystal clear on your strategy as to how you are going to achieve what you promise. Any investor will quickly see through any bullshit.

Things then move on to constructing a deal. Your advisor will be on hand to help guide you with both the valuation and the deal offered by the prospective investor. For this stage of funding, valuations are based on revenue multiples and growth rates. Later stage deals will be multiples of margins and, later still, profitability metrics.

A valuation is moderately straightforward if the company has achieved traction already. If you haven't, the figure will almost certainly be way under market. Roby warns that while there is the odd crazy story where people have achieved vast amounts with no revenue, they are scarce.

The easiest, cleanest and best deal is when there is an offer of ordinary shares. All the shareholders are equal. However, some investors insist on preferred equity shareholdings, which, in essence, means they get special treatment. These preferred terms may mean they get a higher rate of return or that they get their money out and still retain shares. In addition to ordinary and preferred shareholdings, there are many other structured deals, including convertible notes and debt instruments. Your advisor will make sure you understand these, as and when required.

When people are buying into your company, you should expect them to carry out due diligence before progressing with a deal. This procedure means they will look in depth into every aspect of your business to assess the risks to their money. For this reason, Roby cautions, it is essential that from day one of your business, you keep everything entirely above board. If due diligence reveals something untoward, it could destroy your hopes of obtaining an investment of millions and you never know if you might need this in the future.

One of the biggest challenges surrounding raising investment is that you are giving up a chunk of your baby. To achieve a happy and constructive way forwards, you may need to change your mindset. Roby advises rather than focusing on the loss of your slice of the pie, concentrate on how much of a large pie you will have a slice of. See that going ahead will result in the overall pie being a lot bigger. His final words of caution are that funds at the early stage should primarily be used to invest or support growth. The majority of the funds should be allocated towards growth opportunities such as marketing or further investment in technology. Investment partners who understand this are the ones you should consider working with.

Key takeaways:

- Always use an expert advisor from the start when raising money;
- If you have no numbers yet, expect an under-valuation;
- Be prepared to give up your baby. Don't underestimate how tough this is.

PART THREE

Leadership and Team

People are possibly the biggest of all the challenges to scale. And that includes ourselves. It is incredibly lonely at the top, unless we are blessed with saint-like partners or families combined with the ultimate leadership team.

My own experience was that it was reasonably easy to keep a tight team up to the £1m mark, where everyone was on the same page, we all had great fun and I was able to be near the sort of leader I wanted to be. But I fell headlong into the classic trap of panic recruiting, where you take on people to fill orders rather than team fit and ignore the screams from your gut that you have made a catastrophic error. In Part 3, Natalie Lewis talks about the way one rotten apple can destroy an entire team culture, and it is entirely accurate.

In addition to recruiting great people, you also need to keep them. Adrian Kingwell talks of how the costs of continual recruiting nearly put him out of business and how he developed ways to retain his team to well above industry averages. Rob Hamilton built a company that was not only hugely successful but also regularly winning awards for its culture, and he shares lessons in leadership. With more companies having changed to remote working during the pandemic, and now planning to stay that way, who better to consult than Ranzie Anthony, who has been running teams on three different continents and now adapted to remote working practices for his whole team? But none of this will work unless you learn to look after you and develop the right support team, something else I failed at massively. We'll begin with the wonderful Dame Shellie Hunt, who has coached people at the highest pinnacles of business and tells us how to form the right support team.

11

Your Support Team

Dame Shellie Hunt, Success by Design,
Women of Global Change

DAME SHELLIE'S STORY

Shellie Hunt grew up living under a house in Boston, Massachusetts. Humble beginnings for a woman who would one day earn the title of The First Lady of Entrepreneurs and be recognized by three different US presidents. They lived in what her mum euphemistically called the basement apartment, a cement area under a house padded out with foam flooring tiles. The cement was bone-cold in the Boston winters. She had lots of love but only one pair of shoes at any one time. Part of her is still that little girl who would wait excitedly for a trash bag of used school clothes.

Her parents parted ways while she was still very young, but her mum was a 'firecracker', determined to get them out of poverty. She had nowhere to wash Shellie in the 'basement', so she got hold of two open bags of cement and some old tiles and constructed a three-inch tub. 'Her need to wash me was greater than the obstacle. My first memory of entrepreneurial behaviour. Entrepreneurism is all about how you approach things,' says Dame Shellie.

As early as five, Dame Shellie was also asking questions on life's journey that were beyond her mum's reach. Her mum's best friend had a date who introduced her to Alexander Everett, author of *The Genius Within You*. Everett had formed the Potential Foundation for group transformation and founded a company called Mind Dynamics. Up till this point, work was done one-to-one with little done in group work. Many future stars understudied Everett, including world-renowned motivational speaker and coach, Bob Proctor, with whom Dame Shellie was to form a lifetime friendship. Still only about six years old, Shellie became part of Mind Dynamics, gaining a group of incredible mentors. She learned how the neurons in the brain tune into different frequencies and of our alpha and beta selves – the alpha being primarily concerned with moralistic self-enhancement and the beta with egoistic self-enhancement. She also started meditating for a couple of hours daily.

At 13, she had a terrible riding accident when her horse fell on top of her. Her left wrist was bent back to the elbow, her spleen was bleeding and her left leg shattered. In the long wait for her mum to return to town, the hospital took X-rays and told her she would always have issues walking and would never be able to use her left hand again. Undeterred, she refused the painkillers and practised the techniques she had learned.

During the surgery, the orthopaedic surgeon initially complained the nurses had given him X-rays of a different child. Her body had already changed so much. She emerged with full use of both her hands and legs and attributes this to her use of her mind on her body. From her early work with

Bob Proctor, she had absorbed that while she lives in a body, she is not that body, but thought, emotion and action. This experience showed her how powerful the teachings were.

By the time Dame Shellie recovered, her mentors had gone their separate ways. Still at school, she knew that she wanted to be an entrepreneur, but had never heard the word. She took a succession of jobs, from shovelling horse manure to working behind a reception and in a factory. At an Italian furniture company, she moved up the ladder fast to oversee six warehouses and five stores. But when her boss insulted her, she quit – her first time taking control over what was said to her.

She started to do success training sessions and work that was similar to what Tony Robbins was doing in his coaching and training in the 1980s. She would wear a suit and have her hair in a bun, but weekends found her in sparkly singing gear, working as a professional singer, which she had done since she was 15. When her daughter was three, she finally started her own company. Excited and terrified at the same time, she wondered how, as a single mum, she was going to survive.

Dame Shellie went on to build a succession of companies, up to five at one point. These included Success by Design, which has worked with more than 10,000 individuals, from blue-collar to CEOs and Supreme Court judges, and countless Fortune 100 companies. She has served on many boards, is a lead mentor in the Billionaire Adventure Club, judged the Gracie Awards, hosted the EMMAs and teaches in universities and on business programmes. Her personal life, she believes, is sent to her to keep her humble. She told me that she has experienced rapes, muggings, a home invasion and extreme levels of domestic violence, which she thought would kill her. Dame Shellie has sat on the floor and cried, but

she has always got back up, unbroken. Her experiences have
led her to where she needs to serve, working with rape victims
and children in suffering. She is a legendary philanthropist,
best known for founding Global Women of Change. This
community aims to bring hope and peace worldwide and
has received four consecutive White House awards, multiple
commendations from the United States Senate.

It began when she was visiting Fiji and saw children
grinding corn, so happy despite having so little. Rather than
just asking people for money, she wanted them to be involved
and to act as agents of change. Dame Shellie invites people
to five-star resorts on condition that they spend one day out
in the community to see for themselves what is going on and
how the majority of the world is still surviving on less than a
dollar 25 a day. She received the 2013 Humanitarian Award
at the World Congress Center.

A year later, Dame Shellie was invited to a ceremony by
the Knights Hospitaller. On arrival, the cardinal asked if
she knew why she had been invited. She did not. In fact,
she was then awarded a knighthood by the Order of St
John, joining other luminaries, including Bono, Bob Hope
and Elizabeth Taylor.

Dame Shellie's definition of personal success: *'I sometimes
ask myself if I have really helped people. My definition is
my daughter, who is an additional gift in this world. I hope
that maybe one of the people or children I touch will go
on to become the next leader for peace or discover the cure
for cancer.'*

MENTORS AND YOUR SUPPORT TEAM

Dame Shellie believes we have now become too obsessed with the destination and should enjoy the journey more. But in seeking success, she says that knowledge is never the problem. You can find out for yourself anything you need to know if you are willing to give it a go.

Anyone can become successful; successful people come in all colours and from all walks of life. Success lies in overcoming the limiting beliefs we pick up and reverting to our childhood ways of authenticity and openness. Dame Shellie talks of how she overcame society's training that she wasn't pretty and she was also poor.

At the start of her career, Dame Shellie says that she spent much of her time thinking about failures until eventually, she realized that she should focus instead on what she was doing right and what other people did that brought them success. This concept is where mentors come in and this is Dame Shellie's advice on them: you have to learn from people who are doing what you want to do successfully. Ask what the three biggest things they have done right and the three biggest things they didn't do are and what their three biggest assets are. That, she says, is the shortcut to success – simply ask them. A true mentor will want you to succeed. Indeed, a great one will want you to supersede what they have already achieved.

Go to a mentor in any specialist area, but don't expect them to be a genius in everything. If someone is exceptional at sales, for example, it doesn't mean they have the rest of their lives in order. We are all good at some things and not good at others. In Dame Shelley's case, she says she is not great at maths, but she has 40 years of training and experience in understanding how minds work. Never make the mistake of expecting people to be an all-round genius, even if they come across that way. Get mentored on the area they excel in but don't hold them accountable for not being together for other areas of their lives. Equally, Dame Shellie says that mentors should be responsible and never mentor outside their areas of expertise.

It is an easy trap to fall into to reach out to those closest to us. When she was starting, Dame Shellie's close circle was single mums but the problem is that within your inner circle, you don't get an alternative paradigm and when people reject an idea outside their norm, you internalize that and believe it is impossible.

To work successfully with a mentor, you have to be coachable. You should not expect to understand everything and don't make the error of questioning everything. Trust and surrender to their knowledge. The more you surrender, the more you will succeed. Mentors are imperative. But before you start seeking a mentor, you have to work out what you want from your life and, therefore, what you want from them. People make the mistake of saying, 'When I get the job, I will dress for the job'. Instead, they should say, 'I will dress to get the job'. Being successful in business doesn't mean you are automatically a great leader; leadership takes understanding, relationship building and mentorship.

Misery and excuses both love to camp out together. Dame Shellie warns of the danger of toxic people. Toxic people drain you. Studies show that just one can reduce the performance of an entire company by 40 per cent. Dame Shellie has an agreement with her assistant that if she runs into someone exceptionally toxic, she pulls on her earring and her assistant knows to come and rescue her. She immediately goes outside, kicks off her shoes and walks in some grass to reground herself and clear the bad energy. We have a renewable source of passion and energy that we can tap into, but we forget it exists in the negativity we absorb as teenagers when we start to believe we cannot do things. In our own ways, we all need to kick off our shoes in the grass and get rid of the negativity.

As a leader, you need to surround yourself with people who are good at what they do. You cannot micromanage everything yourself. If you have a great accountant, let them be the accountant. If you have a great visionary, maybe put them in marketing. People want to win, so let them. Also, look for those aligned with your mission and brand.

Find out what motivates each of them. We all need to have motivation and rewards, be it money or recognition, or we go to the side and don't feel we matter or can win. We human beings are communal creatures who want to belong in groups. A leader's job is to both reward and make people feel they belong. You also need to let them speak out without fear. Be the leader who holds the context – we all want someone to be a leader.

Dame Shellie believes that leadership is also about 'inspecting what you need to inspect'. While she does not believe in micromanaging, it is a balance. In the long run, the leader is responsible for managing their team and cultivating the greatness in the individual members. She believes that this is achieved by setting clear expectations and leading by example.

Develop a culture grounded in honesty and self-awareness. For example, if a leader asks one of their team to complete a task that isn't suited to them, they need to be enabled to say so honestly, ask for help or a change of assignment. That honesty benefits both the individual and the team. A strong culture also recognizes the need for having breaks, for them and for you. Resting or quitting should never be thought of as failing, but simply viewed as a sign that you have reached your limit and it is time to stop and take a reward for the hard work. Dame Shellie teaches that we need to understand that each and every one of us should be a leader in our own lane. When a group figures out which lane each person should be in, they can then respect each other.

Key takeaways:

- Work out where you want to go;
- Seek mentors who are expert in one field, not in everything;
- Surround yourself with experts in their own lanes.

12

Running Remote Teams

Ranzie Anthony, Athlon

RANZIE'S STORY

Ranzie Anthony had the unenviable task of discussing tech with me – very brave, given my technophobe tendencies. However, he has the great skill of talking clearly and calmly, and in such simple terms that I completely understood every word. I am sure this skill is part of the secret of his considerable success. He and his partner, Rob Kennedy, run Athlon, a global design and innovation company. Athlon currently has approximately 70 staff, spread over offices in Sofia in Bulgaria, Toronto, New York, Perth and London. They help brands use digital technology to reach their individual business goals.

Ranzie grew up in Stratford, East London. His earliest foray into entrepreneurship was running and selling his school newspaper. He also did some freelancing to supplement his income during university. Ranzie and Rob studied graphic design at Kingston University and were among the few people on the course who were interested in interactive media. Most were keen to focus on traditional brand and editorial design aspects of the course.

When he graduated, Rob went to work for Microsoft, while Ranzie took a role at a design start-up called Deepend, a product of the dot.com boom. They were incredibly fast-growing, going from 11 to 350 staff in five years. But when the bubble burst, they went spectacularly bust.

At that point, digital design and branding were in their infancy, so Ranzie decided to co-found his own company, named Tonic. He had watched what went on at Deepend, and thought he could probably do it too, and was undaunted despite having seen the worst outcome. Over 12 years, Tonic grew from two to 50 people with some massive clients, including Vodafone, Sony, MTV Europe and the British Council. In the end, he sold the company to an international corporate consultancy called College Group, but continued working there for two years. It is often requested that founders stay on for a while after a sale, to ensure smooth handover. Ranzie says he learned a lot from those two years, but that it became a very different culture from the one he had created and it did not feel a good fit.

Rob, meanwhile, had moved to Greece with his family. He was working out of Athens and established a tech development team in Bulgaria. Bulgaria has been very strong in its technical development and these days, many major corporations base their development centres there. Back then, it was mostly untapped. Ranzie had been consulting for a couple of years when the two got together again and decided to set up a new design-focused business.

Their new agency was called Athlon, a merger of Athens and London, being built out of the Bulgarian technical offering. Ranzie set up the London office and Athlon grew, starting to work directly with clients. They were soon gaining business in New York, so they agreed that Rob would move out there and set up a separate office. After three years, they could see that the transitory nature of the New York workforce was giving them issues. As they also had several clients in Toronto, they re-organized. All the design and production became Toronto-based, leaving just Rob and a smaller consultancy team at the New York office.

Timing has helped their success. Digital has gone from being niche to more mainstream and fully recovered from the dot.com boom and crash. Ranzie feels that in the last five years digital technology 'has really come of age.' They have been able to self-fund throughout their growth. While undoubtedly it would have been quicker to grow with investment, overall, Ranzie thinks that using your own money makes you more conscious and more decision focused.

Athlon's most significant challenges have lain in working across borders. While it can be cost-effective to use developers and designers in low-cost locations, there are other problems involved. These have included getting people to employ similar processes, share the same values, adopt similar attitudes to client service and overall achieve the same cultural fit.

There were also the time-zone challenges. With only Rob and one other person in the US for a long time, everyone in London had to work late every night to fit in with the American markets and service them. When Athlon set up in Toronto, they envisaged running a global team, but it turned out that the time zones made that inefficient. A lot of their growing pains have been to do with achieving efficiency on a global, and remote, scale.

Ranzie loves the autonomy of having his businesses and would never do anything else. We discussed and agreed how doing so makes you virtually unemployable as you become so used to making all the decisions. Athlon's decisions continue to drive them to global success, with an office in Australia having launched in January 2020.

> **Ranzie's definition of personal success:** *'For me, it's autonomy. The ability to work with people you enjoy working with, both team and clients, to work where you want. I love the global aspect of our business, that can take us to Toronto or Bulgaria and all the different perspectives, clients and challenges that brings.'*

REMOTE WORKING

A combination of his knowledge of tech, and the fact that Ranzie had been running global offices pre-pandemic, meant I had every confidence in asking his advice on best practices for remote working. For the London office, they already had an 'opt to work from home policy' in place.

Some companies find this trend more challenging than others, depending on how tech savvy they are to begin with. When I first talked to Ranzie, we had been discussing the vast changes in tech and market trends over the last 10 to 15 years. Even pre-pandemic, we lived in a digital world, connected in all sorts of ways, be it by phone, tablet or smart TV, and that means every company is affected.

Ranzie says that every business now has to look at embracing tech to streamline their processes or gather data to make better decisions and/or to deliver better customer experiences to make them competitive, and now the majority have to adapt to remote working. He was explaining to me that technology is becoming increasingly commoditized with more and more off-the-shelf solutions and cloud-based platforms. Using consultants has become much more common and you can now look worldwide for the right one. Good tech partners always start by thinking through the customer experience and what precisely your business goals are. Technology will continue to evolve and change to meet the challenges as they arise.

A good consultant who helps you with both the customer experience and your efficiency should now be considered essential for every company, in the same way as they would have an accountant. At one end, this might mean the provision of off-the-shelf tech, and at the other, it could be a robust ecosystem of platforms to interact with customers. Neither needs to cost massive amounts, but both will help your business, your customers and your team.

As a tech company, this hasn't been Ranzie's challenge with running remote teams. His experience has also revealed that with increased numbers of people working remotely, the work levels were not the biggest concern. It is the company culture that is in danger. He finds it works best if you divide the remote teams and appoint a local office head to the team. They also tend to form team groups to work on particular projects, re-forming again for a new one.

Ranzie has found that what works best for remote UK teams and overseas offices is to focus the people on outcomes rather than tasks. This management style was something they always had practised globally, but it worked so well that he expanded it back to the UK. A new management style comes into play. How people spend their time or when they do the work ceases to be important. What is relevant, and how work is now assessed, are your results and outcomes. There is much less micromanaging and the remote staff benefit from greater freedom and control over their lives.

With a global team, Athlon build culture with regular inter-office meetings and a worldwide team meet once a year. Team events have had to evolve to work effectively remotely. The monthly and annual all-company get-togethers and knowledge-sharing initiatives are critical to the creation of the culture and mission. They have had to adapt to working across multiple time zones. They encourage everyone to take coffee (or water) breaks and have scheduled times when people can take these in a video meeting room and connect informally to others.

The secret is to establish the right balance of checking in with people. Ranzie checks in with his London team daily, monthly with global teams. His direct reports are weekly. Project team meetings happen every day, when required. It all results in an increased amount of liaising time for leaders to keep that culture and work focus strong.

Every day kicks off with a scrum meeting, a 15-minute session where they discuss priorities that need any co-ordination. There are also team kick-off meetings, at the start of a project, where roles and responsibilities are assigned. Ranzie recommends using Slack for internal comms, emails for clients and formal comms, and Zoom for video conferencing. They also use Google Docs and Figma and Miro for real-time collaborative design tools. Ranzie also uses digital tools such as WhatsApp and Slack, where they have specific channels for topics ranging from #embarrassingphotos to #random, with the emphasis on social content to help build relationships.

Tech is now known to be one of the major stress factors in remote work. Everyone has laptops and their systems are Cloud-based, but they also ship monitors and chairs to team members.

On-boarding is much more challenging with remote working. When Athlon have new starters, they ask the newcomers to introduce themselves via a First Thursday all-company video call and they are encouraged to focus on their background and personal interests.

Ongoing learning and personal development have to be as robust as they would be in a traditional office base. Traditionally, they used a buddy system where by team members shadow someone else in the office to help with their development. This system has evolved into a similar system for remote working. They use online learning software packages for training and senior members of staff work with coaches.

The balance between trust and monitoring is perhaps the hardest thing to hit when working with a remote team. Ranzie has refined his recruitment profiles. They now look for people who can be autonomous but are also completely comfortable about asking for help when it is needed. He says this means that they are pivoting more to hiring experienced people rather than those at junior levels.

The policy of trust has always been essential and they try to adopt this first and foremost. Ranzie and his management team only monitor people closely where there is a specific concern or an important project that requires senior team oversight.

Key takeaways:

- Have both a formal and informal structure of regular meetings;
- Move work to be outcome-based;
- Forget micromanaging and develop a policy of trust.

13

The Secrets of a Successful Leader
Rob Hamilton, Instant Offices Group

Rob Hamilton started Instant Offices when he was only 24, but his determination to have his own business started earlier. For a few years prior to that, he had carried a notebook around with him, full of possible business plans, some more realistic than others – he still has it.

As we chatted, I discovered that a defining moment had come for Rob with his A-level results. He had gone to an incredibly academic school, where around half of every year group attained places at Oxbridge. When the results came in, he was a long way from that top half. He felt like a loser and vowed to always try his best at all endeavours in the future.

Rob wanted to study business, but his father persuaded him that a course focused on a speciality would be more useful. He therefore studied commercial real estate management. It was to prove helpful advice. While there, he tried out money-making ideas, including hiring nightclubs and selling tickets. It was his first experience of marketing, doing business with dodgy operators and door-to-door selling. He and the same two friends also tried to set up a mountain bike T-shirt company. This venture was less successful, selling just a handful of items, and he only threw out the last boxes recently. He says both experiences taught him a lot.

From college, he went to work for the banking group BNP Paribas for a couple of years and then on to Chapman Swabey, working for a small owner-managed business. He continued to work on business ideas, considering a soup and juice bar, which had become popular in New York, but the start-up capital was too high. Rob was haunted by the idea that if he left starting a business until he was 30, he would by then have a wife and children and never begin. He says he is too risk-averse. But equally, he was desperate for independence and convinced that he was not very good at working for other people and would never get far like that.

Rob went to his boss and said that he wanted to start Instant Offices, which was to specialize in letting serviced offices, having finally settled on this idea. He could start Instant with relatively little capital and could see how he could trade quite quickly. His employer put in £20k and Rob added another £10k borrowed from a credit card. It was as lean and low-risk a start-up as possible. He still believes in choosing to start lean in business and thinks the ability to do this is getting lost in today's culture. If you have very little, you can't make lots of expensive mistakes, and learn to protect your downside risk.

Rob had to focus on both sides of the market: the companies that operated all the flexible offices in the country and potential tenants. Starting with finding the landlords, he spent four months sitting in his office creating as detailed a database as he could. He then wrote to them all, announcing, 'I am now working for you; these are my terms of business, please write to me if you don't agree.' It was a win-win for the potential clients, no risk involved, as Instant only got paid when they successfully found a tenant.

To find tenants, he set up partnerships with old contacts, used the *Evening Standard* and advertised in the Yellow Pages. He had a basic website that generated some business through search engines. By his second year, there was Google advertising. His reputation was solid, so people were happy to work with him. Rob says that at this point he had no experience of anything – managing people, marketing or finance – so everything was trial and error.

Timing was key. Rob had spotted a gap in the market for companies that were looking for short-term office space. Regus was still the big player, but most of the potential was still unrealized. Mark Dixon, the founder of Regus, had a tough reputation, but Rob found him 'extremely decent'. Whenever they met, Mark talked about buying Instant, which always gave Rob a confidence boost, demonstrating that maybe they were building some value.

It only took Rob nine months to pay back his investors. He is exceptionally proud that all the expansion that followed was always self-funded, in good and bad times. They went through a couple of bad years following the dot.com bubble bursting in 2001, but with his team's support, they got through it. The year 2003 was a big year; Rob started to expand into the US and Australia, creating a corporate sales team, and began a new division of the business, creating managed offices for large corporates and government. It was to become bigger than the initial idea. Every expansion was risk-averse, low-budget and ready to scale back, if need be. Even the overseas expansion began by running round the clock on different time scales, based in the UK. Overseas offices came in 2005.

Rob told me he didn't have any contacts when he started. Later, he had a friend who founded the DVD rental business LoveFilm. LoveFilm white-labelled their film service to the easyGroup. Rob emailed easyGroup's founder, Stelios Haji-Ioannou. Stelios came straight back and the easyGroup partnered with Rob to white-label the Instant service to easyGroup's customers. Rob says the partnership was not especially good financially, but the PR, with pictures of himself and Stelios everywhere, was terrific.

For 12 years, Rob and his management team built up the company, by which time he was bored with the same old problems coming around again – demanding customers, tech upgrades and so on. He recruited an external CEO and stepped down as CEO in 2011. In 2012, he sold a majority stake at a valuation of £26 million.

Rob's primary concern on selling was for his team, especially senior management. It proved to be well-founded, as he saw first his CEO, then the financial director and then both MDs leave within 18 months. Only a few of his team are still there and it is very corporate now. What he did not anticipate was that litigation was brought against him, claiming that the accounts were inaccurate. It was a great surprise to him as he had never had any serious legal issues or even an employment tribunal is the preceding 14 years. In the following three years, he spent many months, and £100,000s, defending the claim. He sold the remainder of his shares in 2018 in a secondary buyout to Bowmark Capital at a valuation of nearly £90m.

These days, Rob is an Angel Investor with a broad portfolio. His charity work includes Ride25, which he formed with a friend, John Readman, to raise money for the African charity, 1moreChild. In 25 legs, the cyclists are completing a journey from the UK to Australia, but most importantly, now he has time to spend with his family.

Rob's definition of personal success: *'Having a family life. Time and resources to enjoy your family, enough funds, and time to enjoy things with them. I have more time now so I can do a lot of school runs, go to all the different things they are in and have lots of adventures with them.'*

LEADERSHIP

In 2011, Rob was quoted in the *FT* as saying that 'the customer is not always king, the people are.' Everything I read, and every conversation I had with him, made it clear that for him, this is the primary factor in leadership. Instant won innumerable awards for its workplace culture, and was regularly listed in the *Sunday Times* Best Companies. It was also an incredibly successful company, so I asked Rob to tell me more.

He says that he believed in giving people a pleasant environment and autonomy. His first principle was to treat people fairly and be completely open and transparent about their plans. He and his management team always had a clear vision of where they were going and it was equally vital that the whole team knew where they were going, too. They usually worked to a three-year plan and this was summarized on a detailed one-page plan that everyone had. The main goal would be at the top and every area and individual goal set out below; they even included their charity work. They had a simple rule that they could all use – if what you are doing isn't something to do with the plan, don't do it.

Rob says his people enjoyed working hard to get the work done, but this was always mixed with plenty of fun. He also actively discouraged them from working evenings or weekends and says he would never have rung someone on the weekend. Rob is a firm believer that the leader has to be fresh to lead well. He ran his own life on a 12-week programme similar to school term times, with rest and holiday in between. For him, this approach wins every time, resulting in him getting more done and enjoying it more, too. Each 12-week section feels like a race to achieve what you wanted in that period.

The company had a Minister of Fun and organized regular sessions going out together, including competitive events, so it wasn't all about drinking. These went from carpet bowling to an evening competition of *Strictly Come Dancing* with some of the BBC cast. Rob also took the whole company skiing for three days every year, which encouraged people to get out of their comfort zones and try different things. They had 'golden tickets', which were a broad selection of goodies from a dinner out to a plane ticket, awarded to several individuals each month who had done something exceptional – all nominated by their peers.

Another team bonding rule was that every day in all their offices globally a different person would take a cup of tea and a piece of cake to each of their colleagues. As the company grew in London, this ritual would take a good chunk of someone's afternoon, but it was time well spent. Rob and the rest of the management team always took part in the tea round rota. All of these principles and ideas can be adapted to suit remote teams, too.

I asked him where he found his team. He already knew his most important hires, both the MDs of the two sides of the business. Generally, they looked for exceptional staff, tending to avoid hiring people with a corporate background. The quality of recruitment radically improved as they scaled and their reputation grew. The only place where they struggled was the US. A lot of UK staff had to work late to support them at the start. Australia was easier – Rob found that if he offered one of his team the chance to go out there for a year, they would leap at it.

They had a notice that read 'Keep the Jerks Out' and one way they did this was to invite potential recruits to spend a day with their new team. The team would then decide if that person was right. They had a fair pay policy from the bottom up, paying juniors above the going rate. Senior staff, Rob included, were never paid more than £60k basic. This policy meant that some high-level people took a drop in salary to join, but there was the potential to earn much more, both in OTE (on-target earnings) and through getting equity/share options in the business. To Rob, this meant that applicants had self-belief in their success and while a few got cold feet, those who joined, thrived. The basic salary rule also kept costs down so they could weather any bad times. Everyone was on a month's notice. Junior-level staff turned over every two or three years, but seniors hardly ever left and the odd one who did always gave him six months' notice regardless.

Everyone knew the plan was to sell at some point. Rob gave his team a mixture of equity and share options, which he says only worked because of this. The shares/options evaporated when someone left and even partners were bought out on departure at a valuation substantially below market value, which created a real incentive to stay and crystallize value from the equity earned. It also encouraged the focus on a common aim. Rob is proud of the fact that despite no one in the company paying for any shares, seven of the employees from his time have crystallized shares worth more than £1m.

Rob was always completely open with his team, down to sharing the open-plan office with them. He held what were called 'Hamilton half-hours', where he sat in a side room and anyone was welcome to come and ask him absolutely anything they wanted. Other senior members of his team would be on hand in case anyone preferred to speak to them. These regular meetings meant there was no room for destructive rumours as people could always find out the truth for themselves.

Even when things were tight for a couple of years, Rob sat everyone down, shared all the figures with his whole team, showed them what they needed to do to survive and what would happen if they didn't. No one jumped ship. Instead, they worked their hearts out and turned it around. He always believed in sharing both good and bad times and was exceptionally open throughout, engaging and listening to people.

Talking to Rob was great, not least because it reassured me that truly decent people can be successful.

Key takeaways:

- Share the vision and, if you are planning to sell, consider share options as well;
- Be completely open and transparent;
- Work hard, rest hard and have a lot of fun – you as much as your team.

14

The Critical Culture Factor

Natalie Lewis, Dynamic HR

NATALIE'S STORY

I had the very genuine pleasure of working with Natalie Lewis for a few years. After a succession of HR people who were more interested in covering their own backs than offering anything constructive, let alone coming vaguely close to understanding the problems I was having, Natalie was always a breath of fresh air. She was fun, she was down to earth, tough with me when I needed it and supportive too when I needed that. I learned a massive amount from her and I was delighted when she agreed to share her own story and how her experiences of toxic cultures gave her the passion that she has to work with leaders to create positive ones.

Natalie's first experience of good teamwork and culture was when she started working in pubs and bars while studying for her first degree. The culture was strong and it was fun and rewarding. Despite the job being being low-paid, the managers knew how to recruit the right people and motivate everyone with fun competitions. After her degree, she went to work in the in-house recruiting part of the HR department in the NHS. It was her first big culture shock and she says she 'soon realized I was very much the black sheep of the department. I wanted to make changes to my role and alter processes and procedures.' Vacancies were taking 18+ weeks to fill, with people accepting jobs and getting bored waiting to start and going elsewhere instead. She identified changes to reduce this to eight weeks, but 'nothing quick happens in the NHS, and God forbid that you want to make changes!' Natalie says that she had soon 'pissed off a lot of people' and her contract wasn't renewed.

She moved to a huge pharmaceutical company, which was very corporate but fast-paced, fun and engaging. It was very money-focused, but staff were treated incredibly well with massive rewards packages. Their recruitment processes were fastidious with assessment centres playing a big part: if you didn't fit the culture, you didn't get in. From there, she took time out to complete a master's degree in human resources and then became HR manager for a hosting company, where she was tasked with setting up HR processes and doubling the staff within the year. She adapted what she had learned to suit a small business, so again applied the rule that if you didn't fit with the values, you didn't get in.

Natalie says this was a work hard, play hard environment. At that time, you had to sell your soul to the workplace. Social lives were frowned upon; if you were awake, you were expected to be in work, especially if you were part of the sales team. The pace was incredible and there were echoes of *The Wolf of Wall Street*-style culture back in those days. She grew weary and wanted to move away from in-house HR so she joined a local consultancy and learned to juggle the needs of 30 clients at a time. The work was fun and challenging and there was a lot of problem-solving involved, which she loved. Sadly, the culture let this company down. It was incredibly toxic. Employees were played off against each other; bullying and relentless criticism were normalized. The micromanagement was stifling. Initially, she took it as a challenge and believed that if she got better at her job, learned more, did more, then the bullying and constant red-penning of her work would stop – it didn't.

The pressure increased, but Natalie was stuck in a cycle of thinking that she wasn't good enough to move away to another company. She was told that she wasn't good enough on a daily basis. Believing it, she stuck it out for three years: 'The stress was unbelievable. I got ill and was on the verge of a breakdown. I had to leave for the sake of my mental health. It was at that point where I decided I was never going to work under someone else again.' But there was a problem: while she had learned a lot, Natalie had been left with no self-belief. She didn't think she had enough experience or that she was good enough. One of her old clients took her out to lunch and told her to 'just f***ing do it!' Six months later, she had set up Dynamic HR Services.

Her plan was to disrupt the HR world. She wanted to support small business owners in a way that gave them as much flexibility and agility as possible. Natalie says, 'I wanted my clients to have options and understand the associated risks with those options, not to have to follow prescriptive processes. I wanted the people in those businesses to feel valued and part of a greater purpose. I knew that creating a strong, positive culture in business was the key to success.'

Over the years, she has developed a system that she calls the Foundations of Success. The core of this system is company vision, values and culture. The rest of the system focuses on systems, processes and, most importantly, bringing the 'human' back to the workplace.

Her experiences made her realize that society has changed: 'Employees want interesting work that makes a difference and aligns with their personal sense of purpose/values. They want leaders who care about them as an individual and they want the opportunity to learn and grow. The youngest of our working generation wants experiences and they want to be inspired. There is a big focus on the quality of life, where the old "command and control" style of management is seen as outdated and the "manager-as-coach" model is preferred, giving employees more empowerment and a sense of control over their work.'

Natalie says that it is with these principles that she now spends at least 50 per cent of her time working with small businesses that have grown too fast and, in doing so, failed to hold on to their company culture.

Natalie's definition of personal success: *'I've always said that I want to inspire people. I want someone to look at me and say "because of you, I didn't give up." My definition of personal success is knowing that what you're doing in life is helping you and others to lead a better, happier and more fulfilled life. In my opinion, real success can be measured by how happy you are and the positive influence you have on others.'*

THE RIGHT CULTURE

Natalie defines culture as both the foundations and the glue that holds a company together and what keeps relationships within it healthy and productive. Without a positive vision and strong company values, the work culture can quickly become toxic. She believes that toxic work culture turnaround is possible, but the quicker the company owner spots it, the faster the toxicity can be nipped in the bud. Natalie and I have talked a lot about culture over the years and the following is her advice.

First, and most importantly, the actual purpose of the business and its values have to be extremely clear to everyone. It is also vital that you have a clear picture of the company culture you want to create and that everything you do revolves around this. Natalie also advises putting processes into place as early as possible because they are harder to change later.

Give your job descriptions maximum clarity and envisage what success in that role truly means, because if you don't know, your employee won't either, nor will you be able to measure how well they are doing in the role.

Natalie says the relationship between employer and employee should always be treated like a bank that you pay into with both positive and negative, the positive being good feedback and thank yous, the negative being criticism. She says it is simple: you should always be on the positive side. Irrespective of less-than-perfect work, you can still say thank you for the effort or good parts, and above all, you can always stop and ask how people are. Thank yous, she believes, are vastly underrated and should be given more often, and more loudly than most companies do. It is often said that employees don't leave companies – they leave managers.

How you inboard them is critical as well. You want new people to feel exceptionally wanted and welcomed from the start. Think about sending orientation packs out the week before they start, introducing them to the rest of the team, alongside other useful information. On the day, introduce them to the company's senior team as well as the people they will be working with, be it remotely or in person. Sell them on the whole concept and mission of the company. Reiterate why it is great and tell them all about the values and culture. Then, and at regular onward intervals, make it clear what is expected of them and why. And, of course, thank them continually.

Natalie works to minimize rules and regulations in HR. She believes that the majority of rules are created as a knee-jerk reaction by management to one person's actions in the fear others will behave the same way. They should talk to that one member of staff, but instead they end up treating everyone like children and causing mass gloom. For most companies inflexible working, nil personal Internet use, set dress codes and no home working are all things of the past, she feels.

In the early stages, it is relatively easy to create a great culture; everyone knows what is happening and why, they know each other well, they know what needs doing, they know the clients and life is full of fun. It is one of the ironies that so often, success is what leads to a toxic culture and, in turn, ends up destroying businesses. The staff become disengaged and unhappy.

Partly, the business owners don't have the time to focus on the staff as they once did. Second, it is through what Natalie describes as 'distressed recruiting disasters'. As Natalie puts it, someone hired as a bum-on-seat solution, who is a bad apple, spoils the whole pile. These people are what leadership coach Nigel Risner calls 'internal terrorists'.

Value both skills and cultural fit. Both the entrepeneur Gary Vaynerchuk and Simon Sinek, of *Start With Why* fame, continually talk of the damage even the top performer can do if they are the wrong type of person. However good their figures, however much people say how well they perform, these people will cause the death of the business. Getting rid of them if they don't fit is the only thing that keeps your company alive in the long run. Recruiting mistakes are expensive, but keeping the wrong person is more so.

Key takeaways:

- Have clarity, be it on vision or expectations, and share openly;
- Inboarding is critical;
- Get rid of internal terrorists, however well they perform, as fast as possible.

15

Innovation for Retention

Adrian Kingwell, Mezzo Labs

ADRIAN'S STORY

Adrian Kingwell grew up in Hampshire, UK. His father and grandfather both had businesses, so there was some expectation on Adrian to have one too, but he had different ideas. After studying English at Loughborough University, he wanted to be a film director, so he studied film and video production in Chicago. By the time he came back to England, he had a wife and child to support so he had to put his movie dreams on hold. He went into sales for the income, finally working for a healthcare recruitment company. Adrian says that although it was a baptism of fire, he learned a considerable amount by watching the founder. However, he hated the culture and vowed that if he had a company, he would run it very differently.

In 2006, at 39, he decided to do just that and started Mezzo Labs. A partner coming in a few years later helped significant growth, but it proved unsustainable. He and his business partner were at different points in life with very different needs and goals. Three years in, they split up the partnership, leaving Adrian free to restructure the company.

Mezzo Labs started as a company that wrote content for businesses, but that was tough. 'Every client thinks they could write if they had time,' says Adrian, 'so it made more sense if we offered something that they knew they couldn't do.' So, they pivoted to providing a more sustainable, higher-value proposition: data analytics.

Writing is something that creeps into our discussions a lot. Adrian's background is all creative and he says he would love to write himself. At the moment, he is concentrating on creating a great company out of his earlier experiences. He gives his team a tremendous amount of autonomy, partly because he believes in it, but also because he is not a data guy. He is a creator, so he concentrates on running the company and enabling their expertise.

Early on, Adrian found himself in deep trouble. Not having access to loans or investors, he bootstrapped the business out of its own cash flow. In the early years, staff turnover was very high. He worked out that it was draining the company by at least 25 per cent of the first year's salary to recruit someone, as they were joining and leaving so fast, and that the company was not going to survive if this carried on.

These high costs were about to put him out of business. Adrian started by looking at the way he was recruiting. He visited a Waterstones bookstore to find a book on interviewing. There were many books on how to be interviewed but none on how to hold one. He muses that this is a book he might write one day. Meanwhile, he had to work interviewing out for himself, consulting a variety of experts and HR people. One of the significant steps forwards, he says, was when he stopped the natural inclination to think, 'I like you, and so I will hire you,' and instead concentrated on skills and company fit. He refined the process, asked better questions, set more challenging role plays. Hiring the right people takes time, he says, but firing the wrong ones takes a lot longer. The team has also chosen the brand values of generosity, empathy, drive, 'wow' and spark.

Adrian is a great believer in challenging the status quo. He noticed that his customers tend to look at the data for answers instead of first discussing what questions they have. Their 'bottom-up' approach could lead to very restricted thinking and lose sight of anything bar data. The brilliant line on his website, 'less dirt, more diamonds,' is about how they focus on the things that matter and are relevant, rather than drowning the customer in data for data's sake. His mission is to make Mezzo Labs the best analytics company in the world. He has started a three-year plan to sell their own technology as well as services. They have an office in Hong Kong and another in Singapore. Adrian says that the opportunities in the Pacific Rim are great, but offices at that distance bring new staff problems. A skills shortage in Hong Kong meant he had to send out several staff from London.

He couldn't have achieved the success if he hadn't solved the staff retention issue.

Adrian's definition of personal success: *'An affirmation from a third party of having done a good job. That could be a stranger at a conference saying, "I've heard you guys do great things". Or it could be an investor who values your business at more than you were expecting. Those are all affirmations that the business has created value, that customers are happy, that employees are happy and that I have done a good job.'*

RETAINING YOUR TEAM

Go back a few decades and people applied for jobs intending to stay long-term. It wasn't unusual to find people staying with the same company for life. But the employment marketplace has changed. People have learned that jobs in major corporations are not as safe as they appear. Changes in technology quickly make old skills redundant unless they are regularly updated, rather than lasting that lifetime. The workforce adapts to these changes and as a result, is much more fickle, staying only one to two years in each position and relearning their skills as they go. It has all created a workforce focused not just on finding a brilliant culture, as discussed with Rob Hamilton and Natalie Lewis, but in developing themselves for whatever the future may bring. They want to be more involved and have more control of where their lives are going, have more autonomy. They want clarity on their immediate future.

In turn, the businesses that thrive are those that are facilitating these changes. These 'agents of change' create trends, encourage people not to fear failure if it helps them learn. An influential culture develops where it is safe to try things out, safe to be a disruptor at ground level, but also be empowered to take reasonable risks in line with the ability and the ROI (return on investment).

Adrian's solution has been to create what he calls a talent incubator – a promise to each new employee that his company will help them develop the skills that will get them one or two steps up that career ladder. The bet is that the employee, knowing that their employer is committed to incubating their talent, will be more committed to the long term (and so not quit after a year) and will produce better work along the way.

This system is simple when an employee has clear aspirations. The problem is that many don't. Adrian then set about working with a life coach, Sarah Fraser, to produce the Inside Out programme, the framework for identifying an individual's life goals.

The concept revolves around Adrian's belief that we all have a book inside us, but not everyone is a writer. So, he created a book with chapter headings and blank pages beneath each one. Sarah helps each employee to complete their book, define their goals and work out a route to get to them. Everyone who joins Mezzo Labs gets their own Inside Out book on the first day. Sarah then works very closely with each person during their probationary period to start writing the book. She is also on call at any time in case they have work problems that they cannot talk to their manager about.

The approach is a life-coaching one. Sometimes issues that crop up are indeed outside the workplace. For example, it might be that someone has a financial crisis and needs help to see it in perspective and work through solutions. But it is mostly about focusing on where they want to go, which means that people connect with the point of what they are doing, which in turn makes them happier doing it.

I asked Adrian how much this was about training. He explained that while the need for training may become apparent in their work with Sarah, it is not her remit to deliver skills training. If during a session, they decide training is relevant, that person will then request it via their manager. Adrian explains that what used to happen is that people would ask to go on courses without a clear purpose. Now, requests have clarity on the why behind the application, what the function and benefits are. These requests are more likely to win management support as the ROI to both parties will be clear.

I asked Adrian if he ever had training requests that were irrelevant to their career path, randomly giving the example of learning to juggle. He hesitated for a moment. By an uncanny coincidence, it turned out that on a pre-pandemic strategy away-day on HMS *Belfast*, Adrian had hired a circus performer to teach his management team how to juggle and spin plates. The purpose was to show everyone that by breaking an impossible task into small stages, we can achieve way more than we thought. It was a fun and highly motivational exercise.

One of the many benefits of the Inside Out programme is that it divides the soft and hard management skills that are often so hard to perform together. Sarah provides the soft skills, the people-orientated coaching, which frees the managers up to concentrate on organizational and directional skills.

The programme slows down after their probationary period and when the course they want to take over the next few years has been mapped out. A monthly drop-in meeting is on offer for support and twice a year they hold meetings around the six-month reviews. Another benefit is that team members now come into their reviews with a clear picture of both what they have achieved and what they need the company to help them to reach next. An additional benefit is that Adrian will be more aware of any disconnect between the two well ahead of any potential crisis.

Everything that goes on in discussions with Sarah is always completely confidential, with Adrian learning nothing of the content. The nearest it would ever get is if four or five people said something is not working, in which case Sarah might come to Adrian and say, 'We need to have a look at X,' but conversations remain between Sarah and the team member. She also runs anonymous surveys every year to check how the programme is doing. Adrian says that as the costs of the programme rise in line with company growth, there is always the question 'Is it worth it?' So he asks the team what they think – and they quickly argue him out of it.

He explains that if someone has been there two years and is on course to achieve something they are aiming at on a three-year plan, then he knows they will stay another year. By this simple logic, and by having a generally far happier, more focused and more productive team, Mezzo Labs has achieved an attrition rate around two to three times better than the industry average. Given that they have also tripled the size of the team in six years, it is particularly impressive.

The key takeaway from this is that to achieve staff retention in today's demanding marketplace, you have to help employees figure out where they want to go and then support them on that journey.

Key takeaways:

- Focus on staff retention to lower your costs;
- Help employees figure out where they want to go and support them to get there;
- Give them as much autonomy as possible.

PART FOUR

Marketing

Once you accept that a random, sell-anything-anywhere approach is not the way forward to sustainable growth, marketing comes into its own. Up until this point, it may be nothing more than a website and an appearance on social media. You need to understand who your customers are, what different groups they fall into, what they think and feel. You must be able to identify which ones make you money and which ones don't, where to find them and how much it costs to acquire them. You need to understand and develop your value proposition, which incidentally includes your USP, but is the entire picture of what your customer's problem is and how you are answering it and how you can add additional value to them.

Your company's business on the net has become of paramount importance. David Meerman Scott is a leading global expert on how to develop marketing on the net, how it differs from the rest of marketing, and how to develop and retain your customers. George Sullivan has a successful business that is entirely reliant on the quality of content, so who better to explain what genuinely golden content is. Someone who understands all about what is needed to stand out in a crowded marketplace and offer customers extra value is Matt Sweetwood and here, he explains how you can do this, too. But that is still not enough. You need to develop a genuine differentiation to have a proposition for sustainable scalability and Ed Molyneux shares how that can be done authentically. Also in this section is Paris Cutler, who explains her take on how innovators can apply blue ocean marketing strategies to find new markets for their businesses.

16

Marketing Strategy

David Meerman Scott, Strategist, Speaker, Author

DAVID'S STORY

David Meerman Scott grew up in Boston. In his early teens, he had two business interests. One was a grass-cutting business and he also worked in a cheese shop. He was the sole employee and the owner quickly discovered that, with David at the helm, he was safe to go off for hours to play golf or even to go away for a few days at a time. By 16, David was used to making business decisions.

Later, he went to Kenyon College, Ohio, where he studied economics but preferred to party and listen to music. He developed a particular passion for the Grateful Dead and has remained a life-long fan.

David started work as a bond trader, but that didn't work out. He found the information businesses that bond traders were using to obtain their information electronically more interesting and so became a salesperson on Wall Street. The company he was working for asked for a volunteer to work in Tokyo. David put his hand up and shortly after his 26th birthday, found himself in Japan, with no contacts, unable to speak the language and in sole charge of setting up an office there. He stayed in Asia for nearly 10 years.

Back home, he was working in marketing at the height of the dot.com boom with multi-million-dollar budgets, but David focused on creating content-rich marketing and PR to get attraction at a minimal cost. The company was subject to a takeover and, for what David says was a variety of reasons, he got fired.

It was just after 9/11. People were not hiring and the economy was in a poor state. David decided to start his own business. He describes himself as having been 'unemployed ever since' and says he will never have another job.

David built his business to become a sales and marketing strategist of international repute. He has spoken at leading global conferences and on all seven continents. Speaking engagement clients include Microsoft, Ford Motor Company, Dow Jones and Tony Robbins. Each year, he does around 40 speaking gigs. He loves to speak live and draws his energy from it. He also loves the interactions he has with people, both during and after the events. Every day, he gets emails from people thanking him and telling him how his advice and strategies have helped.

David also does virtual work, both podcasts and virtual events on Zoom and some more high-end productions with a TV company. He is a prolific author, with a list of internationally best-selling books that explain his unique ways of building businesses and providing Real-Time tools and strategies. His books have sold more than 1m copies in 29 languages. His book, *Newsjacking: How to Inject Your Ideas Into a Breaking News Story and Generate Tons of Media*

Coverage, was one of the major causes for the rise of that marketing phenomenon. Recently, he created the concept of Fanocracy, explained in the book of the same name, and has written with his daughter, Reiko. He sits on several boards, is a strategic partner with a venture capital fund and has co-founded a sonic branding studio.

Live music remains a huge passion of David's, to the point where he keeps an Excel spreadsheet of the hundreds of live shows he has seen, more than 800 and counting. He has an outstanding home museum collection from the Apollo lunar programmes. He also loves to surf and uses the opportunity of visiting countries when speaking to try out their waters, meaning he has managed to surf from Hawaii to Costa Rica. He is passionate about the environment and offsets the enormous air miles his work necessitates by making a significant investment to help preserve 10,000 acres of rainforest in Panama.

David's definition of personal success: It *'comes when I help other people. It is really important to me and has been during all the 18 years I have done this, be it through my books, my speaking, or social media. Among the thank yous I get daily, just the other day someone told me that they had grown their business to employ 27 people. I thought, that is 27 families I have impacted on. Holy cow, that is awesome! I am not religious, but I am spiritual and believe the more you give out to the universe, the more you get back. I truly believe that. I put a ton of free stuff out there and I get joy back.'*

MARKETING STRATEGY

In the early years of business, we tend to focus on selling everything we can to anyone who will buy. Marketing becomes an increasingly vital component when we start to scale. I started by asking for David's advice on what strategy to apply at this point. He is clear: planning always starts with the clarity of your buyer persona. Only this enables you to understand your customers' problems and their needs. He describes this as 'a short biography of the typical customer, not just a job description but a person description'.

The second part of your strategy, once you have your buyer persona, is to work out how you are going to reach your customers. For most businesses these days that means having a strong online presence and highly effective social media. You can then use these channels to create quality, useful information for your customers. This communication is the essential component of how organizations effectively market.

David explains that the marketplace has shifted away from what he calls 'pushing stuff in people's faces', when it never occurred to people to approach from the angle of being helpful. He says the pendulum had shifted too far into the superficial in both sales and marketing. We all experience this pressured selling. We buy a product and get on that company's email list and are immediately barraged by emails twice a day, trying to sell us something else. We connect to people on LinkedIn and at once, that new connection is trying to sell us something.

Of course, it is valid to ask for an email address at some point. But what people now do is the same as going to a cocktail party and saying, 'Hi, my name is David, give me your business card.' We know better than to do that. We have a great conversation, share a glass of wine, ask about each other's families and interests, perhaps a little about work and then suggest meeting for lunch, asking for contact details to confirm. We never demand it in the first 10 seconds.

David says that everyone is heartily sick of being asked for their personal information when trying to view a website page. Instead, you have to be helpful and give your visitor a gift with no expectation of a return. It might be content or something to benefit the community or the universe.

Organizations tend to make the tactical mistake of forming their communications all about their products and services, repeating what it is that they do and how they do it faster, better, cheaper. The real truth is that people are not interested in your product. What they are interested in is themselves and solving their problems. Companies that are about to scale up need to give some thought to this. They should stop talking about what they do and start thinking about the people they serve. Once they have learned about them and identified their problems, they can then create value for them. Giving value will be the best introduction to who you are and be a far better way of reaching people.

Sales and marketing often converge, particularly online. David says that a simple way of looking at it is that marketing is reaching many people at once, while sales reach only one at a time, but both can use the same approaches. He is a big fan of using videos for both. While there are many reasons videos are successful, a primary one is that our neurons fire when we watch a video and it feels as if the people in it are in the same room as us. This effect is the reason why, however much logic tells us that we are not, we start to think of film stars and people we have never met as people we know. David and

I were chatting on Zoom and he demonstrated this. He had a slice of lemon and proceeded to suck it, describing the taste and wrinkling his nose at the sourness. Sure enough, I started to taste the lemon.

Entrepreneurs can use this great way to connect with people to their advantage. They can create videos and put them out on social media at little or no cost, reaching many people via their websites and social media. They can also create a video for a one-to-one for a specific sales prospect. The science behind the motor neurons' effects and using them in marketing is a critical concept in *Fanocracy*.

David believes video will only grow as we see the 2020s become a kinder, gentler place in which to do sales and marketing. Companies need to get back to real relationships and video is one of the keys. He advises ceasing all 'gobbledegook' language, and buzzwords such as 'cutting edge' and 'best of breed'. Companies should also be removing all stock photos with fake people from marketing, be it print, ads or your website.

It is all-important to start reaching out and treating people as humans. Always tell the truth and be transparent. So many organizations hide behind corporate speak and legalese. If you make a mistake, own up to it – it can make a huge difference. One false start, being caught out in a lie, these things can be devastating for a business. You must never try to take advantage of your customers in a non-transparent way.

I asked David how these changes had impacted on marketing analytics. He says that 30 years ago, when he first started, we measured sales leads, specifically people who came in the door, particularly in B2B. Now, marketing analytics is more strategic. We measure the engagement reach in addition to sales success and revenue generated. Focusing only on sales leads creates a false way of communicating. People then become focused on strategies, such as creating forms to fill in on their websites that demand information. It can be counterproductive when you keep pushing for personal information. Frequently, someone has come to your website just for a first look and that intrusive demand puts the relationship on an adversarial footing – not a great way to generate new business. David believes ungated, free and beneficial content is far more effective. However, he warns that content gets confused with information. Good content informs and educates; you should barely mention what you do in what you publish.

The fanocracy concept came from when David and his daughter set out to discover whether any organization can create fans in the same way as their respective heroes, the Grateful Dead and Harry Potter, achieved. The answer was yes and they found examples in virtually every business sector. David explains that humans are hard-wired to want to be part of a tribe. He can go to any Grateful Dead gig in a 30,000-person venue and talk to someone like an old friend. In a tribe of like-minded people, people feel comfortable and cease to feel vulnerable.

An organization starts with building a tribe of like-minded people and turning them into fans. Fans are a powerful thing, supporting you, buying more from you, returning every year and telling their friends about you. Using fanocracy is an incredibly powerful way of growing a business but when you develop a tribe, you have to realize the fans will take over. J.K. Rowling, for example, no longer has complete control of the Harry Potter narrative. The fans decide how he is perceived. It is the same with a company. People will talk about you in whatever way they want and you cannot control it. The gain is that fanocracy's results can also outstrip any direct marketing because the fans are real people.

Key takeaways:

- Nail your buyer persona; this is the key to your strategy;
- Work out how you can best be of service to them;
- Be authentic, be real and treat your customers the same to create real fans.

17

How to Create Golden Content
George Sullivan, The Sole Supplier

Catching up with George Sullivan, I started by asking him how the filming had gone at ComplexCon in LA during the last couple of weeks. He countered that he had been back a week and had just been working on a podcast with David Beckham, discussing which trainers Beckham has preferred over the years. One of the many great things about George is that he still thinks it's incredibly cool to be doing podcasts with David Beckham and isn't embarrassed to say so. For someone living what many would see as an outlandishly glamorous life among the famous and socially influential, George is down to earth, super helpful and downright nice.

I was intrigued to find out how he used an English A-level and a love of writing to get to where he is. George grew up in south-east London. His father had a traditional print business, which had failed due to the arrival of digital printing. They were, and still are, a very close family. From his teens, George aimed to have his own business of some sort.

George took a job to keep the money coming in, first as a digital media consultant and then in recruitment. His first business was called Explore My Property, which provided videos of high-end properties that needed additional visual aid to show them off. That was more than 10 years ago and he was just fractionally ahead of the game with the concept. Now, using video to sell properties is mainstream.

After that, George had lots of side hustles going on. He bought designer gear and vintage clothing from charity shops to sell on. George had a passion for shoes and started queuing up for new releases. Seeing that the latest fashion brands sold out within hours and could be re-sold at twice the price, he took to buying two or three pairs at a time and selling the spares every week.

Recruitment began to pall and George decided to start an online business of some sort. He stopped drinking and going out, and spent his time reading every business book he could lay his hands on, especially soaking up everything he could about web design and digital marketing. The shoe re-sale business was bringing in some extra cash, but he was finding it frustrating to find out when and where the big new releases would be. Talking to others with the same passion, he discovered it was a common problem: he had spotted a gap in the market.

In 2013, he set up a website called The Sole Supplier. He would write the blogs in his bedroom before going to work or spend his lunch hour doing them. Working from the computer in his parents' study, he built the original website on WordPress. It shared the latest news about trainers, especially when and where people could buy the newest, hottest releases. His overheads were low and he was able to fund everything himself, which was to become more and more critical as The

Sole Supplier grew. Independent funding was the only way to ensure the information he passed on was never biased. They have remained an independent resource so that George only promotes trainers he really believes in.

George told me that six months in, he thought he had hit the final brick wall. He still had his recruitment job, and as he was making no money from the website, he was considering giving it up. Then came what he describes as 'the Golden Day'. His dogged determination finally paid off and he got a number one ranking in Google for the biggest release of the summer, the Nike Air Huarache Triple White. He made several thousand pounds in revenue from the promotion in a day due to the sheer volume of people searching for that shoe: The Sole Supplier had turned a corner.

The business grew from there. George used social media – Facebook, in particular – to form a massive digital community. Members share information but also chat with each other in the same way as he did when he first started, which encourages the growth of the resale market.

These days, The Sole Supplier helps people source trainers from more than 50 different retailers and continues to keep them informed about when and where the new 'high-heat' ones will be released. It is also now an affiliate marketing company for consumers to follow links directly to retailers. The brands, including Nike, Adidas, Jordan and Yeezy, work with The Sole Supplier and provide content and information for the site. George and his team create videos and podcasts about the latest designs, also working with the brands. They also now have an app that shows members of his community personalized selections that they would like. New releases are still bought up and re-sold for two or three times the price within minutes. The market is enormous, now worth a staggering $2bn. The Sole Supplier delivers £20m of retail sales annually.

George is aiming for The Sole Supplier to be the first point of call before the retailer, not just in the UK but internationally. The company are just releasing a tool that will take them a considerable step forwards towards that. Gone are the days of working out of his bedroom. The Sole Supplier has offices in Greenwich and Shoreditch, and he has moved out himself. But the strong affection for his family remains and he has an equally strong commitment to his team. I am left thinking that it is this strong family bond that keeps him so grounded, despite his success.

> **George's definition of personal success:** *'Being in a business that makes me happy. The money is a result of that, and I would like some behind me, but I want satisfaction every day from what I do. I want a good relationship with my family and my girlfriend, time to go to the gym, to travel and have balance in my life.'*

CONTENT MARKETING

I asked George to share his tips on content marketing and he talked me through the following steps that he learned to apply and start driving them where they are today. He says there is a three-point framework for successful content marketing. What you are aiming for is content that is so good, it will spread itself organically. The Sole Supplier produces a mix of organic and paid content, but their success has always lain in their expertise in organic. When the content is good enough and relevant, Google picks it up and directs traffic to the website.

The first point of the framework is to be the first person to share that content and secondly, that you have to have the best version of that content. After you, there will then come plenty of firms that have the same content second-hand. They will all be trying to find a new, original spin, with rehashed but well-designed content, which means yours has to be better than these.

This strategy relies on developing relationships with everyone you impact upon and everyone in your industry. So if, for example, you have an electronics company, you would talk to your customer and to Sony and Samsung, and aim to get exclusive content and put it into deals. George will go to a company in his industry and say that they will publish, say, five pieces over the next six months and 10 social media mentions in return for an exclusive piece of content each month.

Another way of being first is to get to know people within the brands who will tell you what is going on. While it may not be possible to use what they have told you directly, it can still influence what you write and keep you ahead of the game. These are friendly relationships you can develop via social media, and no contracts are involved, unlike the deals with brands or working with influencers formally.

George and his team use influencers a lot as sources of new, original information. They are in constant touch with anywhere between 50 and 100 influencers on Instagram, Facebook and Pinterest. These are a mix of professional influencers, bloggers or just influential people in the relevant business, but it takes more than just monitoring contacts. They work extremely hard to build relationships with them.

George explains that this means always treating them fairly and giving them something, often payment, in return for their tips. He says that people get the mistaken idea that influencers need promotion. They don't; they need to pay their bills like everyone else. The more fairly you treat people, the better the relationship you have, and the better the relationship, the better the information.

George gave me an example of how this can work. One of their contacts recently told them of a new concept store opening in London. By chance, this person had recognized where it was going to be from the shape of the floor plan. George ran background checks, as he does with all the information he receives, but it was completely accurate. This tip-off enabled The Sole Supplier to be the first to release the news that Kith would be opening in Selfridges. The contact came to them, rather than anyone else, with their information, due to the strength of their relationship.

If you can't be the first, be the best. Being the best is the second part of George's three-part strategy. If, for example, *Men's Health* produce copy about the latest Apple watch, it will be the best initially. However, *Wired*, whose whole strategy is for their content to be the best rather than necessarily the first, will take that content and amplify it. So, if *Men's Health* had 10 points, *Wired* would have 20. They aim to be the very best resource on that topic. You can make an original blog better with additional research, or extra graphics – anything that will add information and value to the reader. Both being the best and being first are very popular strategies. It can become a competitive circle. When the original person sees the improved article, they will go back and take it one more step up. To achieve the best, you need to continually study the competition and learn how to be the best.

The third part of George's three-point strategy is to be original. He has used this a lot. One approach was if, for example, Nike had a sale on, he would put together five of their trainers in an article, which he knows would draw the interest of his readers and save them doing their own research.

They have to be very careful about verifying the information they pass on. George told me that there is quite a bit of 'bad' news out there, often released by people who want to look as if they have more clout than they do in reality. He says that he had to print a couple of apologies in the early days, but now they are alert to it.

George's next point is that you have to be genuinely, passionately interested in the content you are monitoring. He gives the example of one of his developers, who is so passionate about Apple that he chooses to be plugged into absolutely every piece of news about them all the time. His devotion means that he keeps their office up to date with everything they could ever want to know about Apple. He describes his own passion for shoes, saying it has to be an addiction or blind ambition, or both, to obsess all the time. If you aren't that obsessed then find someone else who is.

Start by getting to know your channels. Do this by building up a spreadsheet of every possible news site related to what you do, on every channel, and then begin checking these every half an hour. Gradually, you will start to understand not just what is happening, but where their sources are. You can then start adding in the right social channels and finally, start contributing and become a brand ambassador for that industry. There are a lot of online monitoring tools that can help with all this so that you get news notifications. George recommends BuzzSumo, where you can feed in both key websites and keywords and then be alerted to any news released. Google Alerts notify you when something starts trending. Over time, you will begin to develop your own set of tools and your initiative and instincts to help you spot what is trending, too.

I asked George what his secret to success in the actual writing of the content was. He says it is practice. Do something all the time and you will get better and better. His last tip is based on Simon Sinek's 'Why'. He says you need to ask yourself whether the content is relevant to the 'why' of your mission. Always ask, is that content serving the why in one of those three ways, the first, the best, the original, because if it isn't, you shouldn't write it.

Key takeaways:

- Be the first to share content;
- Create the best version of that content that will beat those following;
- Be original.

18

Understanding Your Customer

Matt Sweetwood, LUXnow

MATT'S STORY

Matt Sweetwood was born and raised in New Jersey. He took a BA in mathematics at Rutgers, State University of New Jersey, and then an MA in theoretical maths at the University of Pennsylvania. Later, he also achieved a PhD in computer science from Warnborough College in Ireland.

Matt met his first girlfriend in graduate school and they married as soon as they left college. Over the next eight years, they raised a family. Sadly, Matt's wife was unstable and often physically abusive. In the end, she left them after a particularly violent episode. Matt recalls the children looking up at him and feeling a massive hole in his heart. He heard a noise far away and realized he was crying.

The divorce was appalling for Matt. The litigation took four-and-a-half years, including a side issue that was taken to the New Jersey Supreme Court. His wife won alimony for life, despite the marriage being under 10 years long. Matt won full custody of the five children.

About five years later, Matt married again, which he says was to a similar kind of woman. After this, he stayed single for almost nine years before marrying again. His experiences in the original case resulted in him setting up The Man Up Project, advising and helping others faced with similar situations.

Matt was facing legal fees of almost a million dollars, alimony and all the while supporting five children under 10. He borrowed on credit cards and sold whatever he could and just kept going. When asked how, he shrugs and says that you stick with it and make it work because you love your kids. For him, that meant working every hour he could and paying the price in sacrificing time that he desperately wanted to spend with the children.

When he had left university, Matt started a business called Unique Photo. He turned this into New Jersey's largest camera superstore, with more than 100 staff and offering the latest in photographic products and imaging technology in addition to the US's largest in-store photography education programme. It grew to be worth several million dollars, due to his radical innovations.

During 28 years in that business, Matt met many challenges, among them being the disappearance of high street stores, emerging digital technology replacing film and the appearance of both Amazon and the Internet.

When he started in the 1980s, they were a B2B (business to business) outlet, selling to small retail and drug stores. While they were the largest photo distributor in the country, Matt's customers were being eaten up by the major players. He took stock of his assets: a strong organization, excellent distribution, great staff, robust dealerships and suppliers. Using those strengths, he pivoted the business from the B2B model to B2C (business to consumer), selling to professionals and consumers. Within three years, they were one of the largest suppliers to professionals in the country. He also used his strong distribution network to sell other products, from health and beauty to racing brake parts. Then, in the mid-2000s, film disappeared almost overnight in favour of digital. Camera stores disappeared. Matt's clients were struggling. Following a gut instinct, Matt created an entirely new type of concept camera superstore in 2008. He put everything into it financially. Within five years, this became the largest single-location camera store in the country and every camera store in the US now runs off a similar model.

Along with the hard work, Matt built all this by understanding his clients. When he created the superstore, he stopped using salespeople and instead used photographers behind the counters, who loved to talk about photography. He treated the merchandise as precious, unlike the old camera stores that allowed their shop layouts to be chaotic and cheap-looking.

Matt knew that having a great store wasn't enough on its own unless he drove customers to it so he added photography classes and made them joyful experiences, taking the students out of the classroom on crazy excursions. Within the first year, 1,000 people were booking in each month. Not only did they bring the store a lot of business, but immediately, customers viewed the staff as their experts and mentors.

Next, Matt went to Canon. He convinced them to loan him one of their best photographers, Art Wolfe, a famous nature photographer. Matt worked like crazy to promote the session, using every sort of marketing he could. When the day came, he had filled an auditorium with 700 people and it brought publicity right across the country.

As his children grew independent, Matt decided that staying in one business for life was not for him. He sold it successfully and set out on his own. His personal brand gave him a good foundation. Already writing for Entrepreneur Media, he transitioned to become a speaker and business consultant. He is also a Panasonic Lumix Luminary, an ambassador for the brand. He became CEO of the beBee – a collaborative social network – a role he held for two years, setting up and overseeing the entire US operation.

Matt is currently the CEO of LUXnow, a peer-to-peer marketplace for exotic and luxury cars, aviation, villas and yachts, all on one platform. He finds time for charities and has been chairman of the board at the Aish Center and the Josephine Herrick Project. He has also written his Amazon bestseller, *Leader of the Pack*, talking about both his business experiences and being a single dad.

Matt's definition of personal success: '*To wake up every day knowing that if I work hard, do things that are right and moral, I can end the day as a success. And of course, seeing my children healthy, successful and contributing to a better world.*'

UNDERSTANDING YOUR CUSTOMER

Given the incredible way that Matt had created his store, going against economic trends and crafting a national retail blueprint, he was the perfect person to ask about this topic. His advice is witty and on point.

Matt says that everything starts by understanding your customer. He often works with both start-ups and scale-ups that have absolutely no understanding of their customers. Matt says that the phrase sounds a bit like a meme now, whereas he means that you must *'really,* completely, understand your customer'.

At the start of your business, you have so few customers and are selling everything to everyone that you possibly can. That may keep you alive and even help you grow a bit, but without a constant stream of customers to form a basis of understanding them from, you still have to prove your business concept and are still at start-up. When that stream turns into a river, you have a business to work on and your confidence soars.

Part of getting to know your customers is to find out what interests them. Not to be confused with what interests you, nor what you *think* might interest them. Matt warns that because so many businesses disconnect and outsource now, it becomes easy for a business owner to disconnect from the customers. To understand them, you have to be hands-on and mix with them all the time. After that, he says, there are many dynamics to be considered. Once you have got some customers, you have to start understanding your customer acquisition model and how much those customers cost you to acquire from the moment they are aware of you right down to the point of sale. You need to test that model to see if it makes sense and is a viable business process. You need to work out how much each new customer is costing you to acquire, which you can do simply by dividing your overall marketing campaign cost by the number of customers acquired. In other words, you can see the return on the investment.

You need to look not just at the number of customers, but how much they are spending to make the figures really relevant. Matt gives the following example: if you are selling bags of bubble gum and they cost you $1,000, you would have to sell a massive amount before you got into profit.

If you adjust the customer acquisition model dynamic, you might perhaps look at selling a bottle of whisky along with the bubble gum and then you will achieve a greater profit from the same number of customers. Knowing your customers means that you can reach them efficiently, modify your business and get more out of them.

One of marketing's most key roles is to get higher-spending customers for less cost and when you scale, this becomes a vital element of your success. You may find that different groups of customer cost different amounts to acquire. A strong customer acquisition model also enables you to start weeding out those customers we all acquire when we start, the ones who cost you more in acquisition, time or energy than you could ever encourage them to spend.

To grow, you need to both retain your customers and create a constant stream of new ones to fuel the growth. It will be tough enough getting new customers without having to continually replace more than you lose via natural methods. Part of working on your acquisition cost is to minimize customer churn and you do that by providing additional value that is of genuine use to your customer.

I asked Matt for his advice on how other people should attack creating something that attracted customers in the way he had. He says solving this is the magic that makes a business successful. You need to know your customers, your marketplace and have the imagination to create a more exciting, more dynamic solution for those customers than anything else around.

Matt told me that there was a time when he wasn't too happy with how his sales staff were doing. The following is what he said to them to explain that magic ingredient of success: 'You have to really care and understand. This store is in a very congested area of New Jersey, just outside Manhattan, and right now, our customer is sitting at home. They have a nice cold beverage and they have their computers on. One window is open on Amazon, the other is open on porn. It is snowing outside and the traffic is all backed up. Our goal is to make them feel they have to put down the drink, close the windows, shovel the snow and get in here because that is what they would rather do.'

Think about what experience options your customer has and make yours the best. Matt says usually he doesn't mention the big names, but it is relevant to talk about Uber here. They created a situation where the customer would think, 'I want to go out, I want to have a drink, so I need to have an Uber.' Need is the critical word, want is not enough. You have to create a need. Matt says yes, Uber is an exceptional company, a unicorn, but there is a lot of space between a unicorn and most start-ups and plenty of room to use your imagination and create that need

---

Key takeaways:

- Mix with your customers all the time to know them;
- Understand your customer acquisition model and optimize its profitability;
- Develop a need in your customer by providing meaningful experiences.

19

Marketing Differentiation

Ed Molyneux, FreeAgent

Ed Molyneux grew up in the late 1970s and early 80s when PC technology was in its exciting infancy and a whole generation of children became today's technologists as a result. However, one of Ed's friends was interested in joining the RAF. In the summer of 1986, the film *Top Gun* was released and instigated a thought process in Ed, although the whole idea still seemed very remote. He borrowed the RAF brochures and started his own application, fully expecting someone to call a halt to his progress at each stage.

Contrary to his expectations, Ed won a sixth form scholarship, which included flying training at a local flying club to get his pilot's licence. The RAF then sponsored him through his engineering degree. After that, he stayed in the RAF as a Harrier pilot for 10 years. He describes his experiences as a real lesson in interdependency. At the start, there is undoubtedly a glamorous and elite image that young pilots expect to have to live up to. That impression lasts until you understand that keeping a pilot in the air for an hour requires more than 50 highly skilled ground crew, upon whom your life literally depends. Ed says the RAF years gave him a unique sense of accomplishment and confidence. When he left, he felt he had already proved himself and that very much impacted his attitude to risk in starting a business. He never worried too much if what he did would work or not.

Ed transitioned out of the RAF as a freelance consultant, working as a technology evaluator liaising between aircrew and software developers. He was also able to spend time with his family and fulfil his ambition of building a house, moving up to the Scottish borders to do so. Ed had developed the first version of FreeAgent in 2006 for his personal use when freelancing. He describes his financial management then as 'pretty ropey' and he was hugely frustrated by his accountant's methods, which required him to type out his bank statement into one of their spreadsheets. Other freelancing friends had the same problem and by 2007, a software specialist, Olly Headey, and designer Roan Lavery joined forces with Ed to develop FreeAgent further.

Ed believes having co-founders is absolutely essential to building something successful. Entrepreneurs tend to have a pathological optimism. They get an idea and model out the exponential growth, arguing that the figures are conservative when, in reality, they are wildly optimistic. They need someone to come along and tell them it might go wrong. Balancing the pathological optimism with a healthy dose of reality is where diversity becomes essential.

Ed says the three co-founders initially wanted to make something a few friends could also use, then got a few more customers and then reached a point of doing reasonably well. At no point did they dream of having a company that grew to 240 employees and more than 100,000 customers or that 13 years later, they would be selling it to the Royal Bank of Scotland.

When I asked Ed what the pivotal moments were, he cites the validation of bringing on board their first Angel Investors in 2010, knowing that others believed in what they were doing. He remembers the silence, but also the sense of promise, walking around their first suite of offices before anyone else got in. Another was being asked by an Edinburgh investment firm what he would do with £1m, should he raise it. Ed says he knew they needed to hire 30 people to spend all that money, but for the first time, he had to work out how that would look in terms of actual job titles and how he might justify the investment in terms of growth.

A Stock Exchange float in 2016 led to a £53m Royal Bank of Scotland takeover. Ed says that by then, they were very clear that FreeAgent's vision was to help people be happier and more successful by putting them in control of their finances. Once they had complete clarity of that central vision, many decisions followed naturally. The RBS deal was, in many ways, just another step along the path towards achieving that vision, giving them significantly expanded access to reach more customers. Ongoing investment from the bank also enables them to accelerate their product development ambitions.

From relatively primitive beginnings, they have expanded from being just an accounting system that helps businesses manage the entirety of their financial arrangements, from connecting to their bank to forecasting their tax liabilities. Currently, they are developing AI systems to provide individual businesses with useful insights in real time. If you are a plumber, for example, they want to be able to tell you what other plumbers in your area are both charging and spending to keep you ahead of the game.

Ed likens investors to the passengers on a bus you are driving. From time to time, different passengers get on (and some get off), but in the end, you are still the one driving the bus and are responsible for its destination and its safety. The job as the CEO, too, has continually evolved. From being the engineer who wrote the first lines of code, he jokes that he has not been allowed to touch the code for the last nine years as they have proper professionals to do that now. Instead, his role is to ensure FreeAgent continually evolves to stay useful and relevant, whatever the economic circumstances.

Ed's definition of personal success: *'One of the reasons I left the RAF was that I wanted to build something from the ground up, something that was mine. What I didn't realize at the time was that a company is actually one of the most powerful ways of creating a positive impact in the world, if done right. But now it is at the heart of what we do. I am very proud of how FreeAgent helps our customers and I view success much more in those terms than in financial ones.'*

AUTHENTIC MARKETING

Ed says advice from entrepreneurs should always come with the caveat that what works for one person in one set of circumstances won't necessarily work for another. He does, however, have several concerns surrounding entrepreneurship and scale to share. One is about the current damaging trend prevalent in tech, particularly, to feel that you ought to be building a billion-dollar company – a so-called unicorn – and aim for enormous venture capital backing or else somehow be seen as a failure. Certain business ideas will only work on a vast consumer scale. But Ed sees millions poured into companies that have no hope of earning them back and where the founders will end up with nothing for 10 years' hard graft, simply because they overcooked what could have been a profitable business.

Many small businesses run incredibly profitably on a modest scale. You don't have to be a superstar and personal financial freedom can come at a lower figure than being a unicorn. It isn't always wise to keep gambling the present for another step up the ladder. Entrepreneurs also often forget that building a business is a marathon, not a sprint. Ed cites Jim Collins's image in his well-known book, *Good to Great*, of a giant Industrial-Revolution flywheel. This vast thing weighs 2 or 3 tons and is 3 metres (10 feet) wide, and in the early days, you are trying to push it on your own, but nothing seems to budge. Then a couple of friends come along and it starts to move an inch and then another in the same direction. After a while, it becomes unstoppable and just needs continual small nudges, each time in the same direction. Business doesn't have to be fireworks and multi-million-pound deals. Lots of little nudges, building up over time, can create massive momentum.

Ed says he used to believe that many people should be entrepreneurs. Now, he thinks that few can sustain the almost inevitable emotional roller coaster, going from the highs of big deals to the lows of fearing you will be out of business by next week. Most people are much more comfortable being somewhere in the middle. He also feels the weight of ownership, particularly everything being your fault when things go badly, can be massively debilitating psychologically. You try to prepare yourself to do a perfect job and instead end up in one where you have to spend a lot of your time making it up as you go along. The emotional and psychological challenges are aspects of entrepreneurship and leadership that are nowadays finally getting a lot more visibility.

Ed says that problems often start with weaknesses in the business idea rather than marketing. He sees lots of founders who fall in love with technology. They build a product and a business around a solution they have decided to offer and then go looking for people with a problem to fit that solution. They struggle to find anyone, especially anyone who wants to pay out any money for it. Ed says that companies need to develop painkillers, not vitamins: the real test is if people will pay for your painkiller.

Many business models are never going to make money because fundamentally, the maths doesn't add up. He uses the example of coffee shops and cafes, which are notoriously short-lived. People think they have a great idea but don't get costs and pricing set up in a way that mean it is possible to succeed. This, in turn, means that someone who has priced correctly further along the same road also fails because they can't compete and you get a wave of failing businesses all in the same market. You need to be very sure that your market is somewhere you can sustain a business at a viable price.

With the marketing you do, the degree you can measure results is hugely helpful. Again, it is tricky for the coffee shop as the only measurement they have is how many coffees they serve. Some businesses do suffer from the adage of 'half my marketing is working, but I don't know which half'. But equally, many companies don't have that excuse. In tech, especially, you have the luxury of being able to test everything you do from the initial point of interest to the final sale, experimenting with what does and doesn't work.

Ed says that word-of-mouth marketing is vastly underrated. It is expected to be essential for a curry house in a local town but isn't people's first thought for a software company. In fact, it does work because word of mouth stands out in the barrage of non-authentic marketing messages. As you grow, the volume of customers referring others can be a significant additional driver of further growth. Good word of mouth also provides reassurance that the customers are happy and everyone, from your investors to your team, gains confidence as a result.

People are afraid of asking for referrals. They think it's not a British thing to do. The trick, of course, is to have a product that people want to talk about and is marketable – it won't work otherwise. Assuming that, if people are good at what they do, present their human side and give people what they want, Ed says it is surprising how amenable people are to doing referrals, especially if you ask them. At FreeAgent, they also offer a small financial incentive, giving both referrer and referee a discount.

From the start, Ed had identified a massive gap in the market where there was no accounting system specifically designed for freelancers. They have always tried to be very specific about who their customers are, deliberately staying away from developing a service for larger companies, preferring to tell their customers to move on if they have outgrown the software. Ed says the key is sticking to customers they understand. He wouldn't pretend to understand the needs of a 20-person manufacturer in Wigan, say, but there is always pressure to move into other markets and keeping true to your customer core can be hard. In the case of FreeAgent, because freelancers are much more like consumers than businesses, it allows them to be more human, have more fun with their language, design style and the way they talk to customers. They can be playful as well as capable and this sets them apart in the world of grey accountancy software companies. From the starting point of knowing and understanding your customer, you have a natural, authentic customer differential from other products and a chance to be very different.

There are only two fundamental strategies you can take: low-cost or differentiated in a way that people will be willing to pay for. But that point of differentiation needs to be backed up by the product, not something that is just a cynical message. We are drowned in messages telling us that things like soap powder are different and it has made people wary. If your washing capsules have three pockets rather than two, it is not enough. Ed says that it's crucial to align behind that differentiation – he doesn't want to be broadcasting a message that a competitor could just as easily say. Then it is just marketing noise. It also has to be framed in the right language and in terms that people will understand. One of FreeAgent's benefits is help on tax returns, but Ed says that if they used 'automated tax software' as a tag, people would immediately think, that is something my accountant does, so I don't need it.

If you know why you are different, it shouldn't be hard to say it and equally to know what to avoid saying. People want to engage with authentic brands. Too many companies, Ed says, aren't, and it does matter. FreeAgent is only able to achieve excellent customer satisfaction scores because they genuinely care and don't just say that they do. People are surprised when they get human and comprehensive responses. It isn't the norm, but it should be.

> ### Key takeaways:
>
> - Beware of scaling for the wrong reasons;
> - Stay true to the customers you know;
> - Any point of differentiation has to be truly different and you have to 100 per cent believe it.

20

How to Spot the Market Gaps

Paris Cutler, Planet Cake and Blue Ocean Strategist

PARIS'S STORY

From as young as six years old, Paris Cutler was sure that she wanted to be this 'something' that we now call an entrepreneur. She spent her holidays hustling in some way. None of her family were entrepreneurs. She had no immediate role models, but as she grew up, Richard Branson brought out Virgin and she followed him and her heroine, Anita Roddick of The Body Shop.

Paris decided against university. All she wanted was to meet entrepreneurs, so she hustled some more, having not gone to private school, to land a job on the trading floor of a stockbroker. There, she met all sorts of entrepreneurs. from inventors to gold miners. She also watched the infamous 'Rats of Sydney' – the delivery boys of that time – on their bikes, whizzing by and not caring if they knocked down old ladies. One entrepreneur saw them as an opportunity. He took them over, smartened them up, gave them walkie-talkies – and made vast amounts of money. Paris realized that this idea of reinventing an old business to develop an untapped market was something she too could do. Meanwhile, she had no capital to consider starting anything, so she decided to study law at the University of New South Wales. Soon afterwards, she got married. Her wedding cake cost her AU$ 1,400 and looked terrible. The customer service was appalling. She recognized this was the gap in the market she was looking for. Martha Stewart was on the rise in the US. Hobbies and homes were on the up.

Paris searched for and found a small cake shop in 2003. It had one employee and no space in the shop for more than three customers, but it was her opportunity to build the lifestyle brand she wanted. She marketed the cakes as a fashion accessory, making them the most expensive in Australia. She went after the high-profile clients and her first was the tennis player, Lleyton Hewitt. Nicole Kidman followed, as did Celine Dion, Rihanna, John Travolta, Katy Perry and Lady Gaga. By 2007, with that brand credibility, they hit their first multi-million turnover, and took on a massive factory with significant capital expenditure and a whole lot of new staff.

In August 2008, the global financial crisis hit. Within three weeks, the phone lines were exhausted with people ringing to cancel their weddings, afraid they would be out of work. Paris believes that the first thing a crisis like that reveals is if you are a leader and able to make tough decisions fast – she was. She had to lay off the staff she had just taken on, one of the hardest things she has ever done. Paris went straight home, downed a vodka and went to bed.

Paris describes how you develop immense fear. For eight months, she was in crisis mode. She slashed overheads and developed strategies to get her through, listing what she could control and letting go of what she couldn't. She learned to stick it out but recognized that she might not make it.

Paris went to everyone she knew, offering them shares in her business in return for capital to keep it going. One person was her landlord, an old-school entrepreneur. He looked her up and down and told her, 'Your business is a dog and I wouldn't want a piece of it in the good times.'

His comment hit her in the gut. 'Is there anything you can do to help?' she asked and so he offered her advice. He asked her to think what piece of her business was the most profitable, not what was doing the best, selling the most, what was the easiest sale. She told him it was the small Saturday courses she was running. He said to her that was where the answer lay and to build from there. She pivoted from being a cake business with Saturday classes to a cake school that also supplies cakes. It became the biggest cake decorating school in the southern hemisphere, educating thousands of students, many of whom went on to have successful cake businesses. *Planet Cake*, the book of the same name that Paris had been writing when the crisis hit, turned into an overnight bestseller, selling half a million copies, and was translated into seven languages. She wrote four more. Suddenly, Paris was everywhere and by 2012, had her own Planet Cake TV show distributed by the BBC worldwide to more than 20 countries. She appeared on the Disney Channel, *The Morning Show*, the *Today Show*, Business News, Sky News, *The Circle* and *Sunrise*.

Paris says she lost herself within the success. She had achieved her goals but had no exit plan and life seemed meaningless. A close friend died and Paris started questioning what it had all been for. By then, she had sacrificed precious time with her daughter and lost her marriage. She thought to herself, 'If I see another cake, I am going to vomit.'

The brand had become so big, it had taken over her life and it terrified her. People were fighting to licence the brand, others urged her to open in different locations worldwide. She describes how people would get glassy-eyed around her and she wanted to tell them, 'Get a grip, it's only a cake.' Her personality became lost in the brand. She recognizes now that this mindset impacted on the business and it started to stall. When she had a success mindset, she succeeded against the odds. Fear imploded in her mind. She didn't believe she had created her success and soon had to realize she also created her downfall.

Paris admits that, like so many entrepreneurs, she made a great leader and a lousy CEO. Entrepreneurs find it easy to take a bucket and mop and build a business out of it, but her own experience has taught her that without meaning and impact, what you do becomes pointless. She finds that the new generation of social entrepreneurs understand that and unlike politicians, will have a positive effect on the world.

Paris sold Planet Cake in 2014. She kicked herself through the self-pity stage, but it took her two years to detox and restore healthy habits and find her way again. Paris knew she didn't want to do brands any more. Instead, she updated her skills and learned social media and PR and loved it. She had another baby and got her mojo back. These days, she divides her time. She does conflict resolution, which she says both 'pays a lot of money and gives her a lot of joy'. She told me of one couple whose business was turning over AU$20 million a year but who hadn't spoken to each other for five years. She also runs a business consultancy service, which includes helping people find new markets for what they do.

Paris shares all the lessons she has learned. She says she has never been a 'skip through the tulips girl' but came to understand that her style of leadership is still a feminine one. When they were in crisis, her natural reaction was to counsel and work with the scared staff, but she was surrounded by people telling her that in a growing business, she couldn't behave like a mother hen and should be more masculine in style. This resulted in a dislocation between who she was and how she acted. Her health suffered and she knows now that this contributed to her burnout. She started to get a reputation for being a bitch. When she works with female leaders, she tells them to be true to themselves and what feels right.

Paris still loves being around entrepreneurs: 'Entrepreneurs are ideas junkies. When you walk into a room of entrepreneurs, no one from the outside would understand the conversation.'

Paris's definition of personal success: *'To wake up every day and do something that I believe betters the world and make money doing that.'*

BLUE OCEAN MARKETING PRINCIPLES

By the time Paris hung up her 'Cake Queen' apron to launch her business strategy consultancy in 2014, she already had a queue of clients knocking on her door. All were struggling to scale and compete in a crowded market. Her clientele includes make-up artists, lawyers, travel agents, property developers and fashion designers. Within a year of working with Paris, 90 per cent of these clients had doubled their turnover and gained an industry leadership position. What makes it more impressive is that Paris often does this on a shoestring marketing budget and only with organic growth.

Paris explained to me that becoming a market leader has very little to do with the quality of the product or service. Surprising though this is, she says that in this day and age, consumers expect a quality product at a fair price. When you compete on that basis, most consumers are left unimpressed and with no urge to buy.

One of her strengths is identifying under-served consumers in crowded markets and pivoting her clients' businesses to market and service those consumers, thus catapulting them to industry leadership in a short space of time. Instead of trying to compete with the other companies already established in the market, Paris looks for consumers who have been neglected or are under-served. This approach means potentially accessing more consumers, with fewer competitors, and in turn, becoming an industry leader.

Entrepreneurs have been using this strategy technique for years. However, it was finally given a name in the book *Blue Ocean Strategy* by Professors W. Chan Kim and Renée Mauborgne. Paris explained to me that Kim and Mauborgne refer to a crowded market as a 'red ocean' and uncontested market space as 'blue ocean'. To be able to shift into blue oceans, they define three key areas: perspective, which requires the right mindset; a clear roadmap and plan; and building the confidence in what you are doing in everyone around you.

All entrepreneurs struggle with finding sales in already crowded, over-competitive marketplaces. This red ocean is where most businesses operate. Everyone is cutting each other up to get business and crying out to become heard in a world where they sound exactly the same as everyone else. In the red ocean, so named after the blood drawn between people fighting over customers, everyone is continually choosing between cost and differentiation.

As Paris explained to me, blue ocean strategists look for an entirely new angle. The aim is to get out of that crowded marketplace and do business elsewhere. To succeed means creating new markets, looking at where the competitors are not selling, what they are not doing. Paris did so instinctively with Planet Cake, making it a fashion brand rather than another wedding cake business, launching a cake school when no one else was doing anything for education in that market.

Blue ocean marketing is for innovators. One of the most famous examples of a company that used blue ocean techniques to reinvent themselves was Cirque du Soleil. They saw the circus dying and rather than struggle in a shrinking market, they created a much more sophisticated audience, way outside the usual perceptions of circuses as a market for their performances.

To reshape a market, you need intensely creative thinking. In the red ocean, everyone is obsessing about the competition and what they are doing. Putting your energy and focus on the others in your market will make you operate like them. Those strengths can be better used to develop somewhere else altogether, looking for new markets.

Using a blue marketing strategy, you switch focus from the competition and run in-depth focus groups on your buyers and consumers. You need to get into your buyers' heads and come to understand what would be of service to them practically and what appeals to them emotionally. At the same time, look for inspiration from other industries. Seek out other people who have turned the norm upside down and learn from them.

The blue ocean approach is to focus on the people or businesses who are not customers, rather than those who are, look at their problems, their pain points and why they don't buy from you and the others in your industry. Before Cirque du Soleil, adults tended not to like circuses because the performances weren't geared for them. They used this pain point to their advantage. Your differentials can be entirely different from your old competitors in these markets. Creating value for your new market is critical.

Some blue oceans are created outside existing markets altogether, while others are about creating a blue space on the edge of an existing red ocean, realigning the boundaries. When you set out to do this, you look at the entirely new benefits that you could bring, a unique style or purpose that is atypical for your industry.

Study how customers in your industry are affected before, during and after a sale. Find a whole new appeal. An excellent example of a company finding a new market on the edge of an existing one was The Body Shop. In the 1970s, they set up in a traditionally expensive skincare and beauty product market whose methods often put luxury needs over ethical considerations. The Body Shop turned the approach upside down, supplying the market with ethical beauty products at competitive prices. They had found people on the edge of the market whose emotional needs were not being met by the old ways.

Differentiation and low cost are both keys in the blue ocean type of marketing strategy. We are trained to believe that there are only two choices: value and low cost. Blue ocean marketing strategies argue you can achieve high value and low cost. In fact, it is crucial. If you haven't nailed the value, it will be easy for the other sharks to swim in. It is also a vital part of the strategy to look at every detail of your company and strip away all unnecessary costs. If it doesn't contribute to the value, it goes. It should be a part of what you develop. The costs for a fashion wedding cake were not proportionally higher than an ordinary wedding cake. The tickets that an adult pays for Cirque du Soleil are massively more expensive than a children's circus.

With blue ocean, another key is to be ahead of the trends. An example of this was Paris spotting what Martha Stewart was doing in the US: she correctly anticipated its spread to Australia. To use innovating marketing techniques, you, too, need to be ahead of the game on trends. Blue ocean techniques focus on creating demands that don't exist at the moment. It is a strategy that needs constant review to keep on seeking blue oceans. Once you have successfully opened one up, there will, of course, be copycats. Blue oceans remain blue only as long as there is no competition and the potential for growth is immense because of its emptiness. However, if you have excelled, you can stay king of your ocean.

Paris explained to me how to identify your undiscovered market. You start by studying your market and industry and identify the weak points. Netflix demonstrates this perfectly. They identified that in the video rental market, most consumers were hugely dissatisfied with the late fees, something no one else had acknowledged. Netflix streaming services addressed this pain point. In the end, they also buried Blockbuster, the video rental stores chain, and the old red market.

Paris underlines the importance of looking at your industry and the market it serves with true dispassion and objectivity. Spot who is not getting serviced in the way they would like. Identify which groups are being ignored and why, and what could be done instead. Find those pain points.

Ignore what the competition is doing. Paris advises you to go as far as actually blocking them on social media. You need to develop a business strategy that will peak in two or three years' time, not a strategy for yesterday.

Key takeaways:

- Collect data, conduct focus groups and surveys to find the pain points;
- Look outside your industry, look at other industries and see what you can adopt;
- Identify companies outside your industry to partner with and help you scale.

PART FIVE

Sales and Customer Relationships

When I was scaling my business, we had a strong sense of what the customer wanted and equally strong lead generation. I genuinely wanted to deliver superb customer service, but to do that, you have to have the right people and the right systems – I didn't.

Andrew Milbourn and I came from the same hard sales stable initially and he reflects here how sales is still a vital function, but it has become crucial to sell with honesty. If the home markets are not enough, Anneke van den Broek shares how she built her business to go global.

An unhappy customer will rarely return a second time, so the customer experience has to be utterly amazing from the get-go. This is something that is all too easy to overlook in favour of concentrating on product, as James Davidson explains. You will want to stand out ahead of your rivals and Sam Kennis reveals how to beat the competition.

While the Internet has made our lives much easier in many ways, it has also increased our vulnerability. Not only are there the trolls that we all have to live with, but reputations can be destroyed, justly and unjustly. For many years, Simon Wadsworth has been an expert in reputation protection and here, he shares where the pitfalls lie and what you can do to protect yourself, and what action to take if the worst happens.

21

Selling with Honesty

Andrew Milbourn, Kiss The Fish

ANDREW'S STORY

I absolutely loved talking to Andrew Milbourn, not least because it was a journey down memory lane for me. Unlike me, Andrew had done a degree in social anthropology but we both ended up with a few years between us applying to work for Haymarket Publishing, which was almost a rite of passage for serious salespeople back in the 1980s. I had to confess to him that while I still remember the interview and the fact that to my slight amazement, I was offered the job, I didn't take it, but went on to work with many ex-Haymarket people in the following years.

Andrew lasted an impressive six years at Haymarket, ending up as group ad manager. It had a very tough reputation and Andrew told me that as a company, it was definitely not for him. It was a very nasty place, he says, with some very unpleasant people around. Andrew told me that in general, however, he was a lousy employee – he hates being told what to do and will always tell people if he thinks they are idiots, another trait I can recognize!

After leaving Haymarket, a friend he had known through the family rang him with a warning that the company he had gone to was about to go bust. This friend suggested Andrew should jump ship and come to work for him instead doing consulting work. Andrew didn't, but of course, the company did go bust. He rang his friend, Don, and asked if the offer was still open. A stockbroking firm was also after Andrew's services and unlike Don, offering a lot of money. After some soul-searching, he took Don's option on a three-month contract, with the knowledge that he would learn a considerable amount in the process.

Sure enough, Don gave him a crash course in consultancy. Then, with fluctuations in the market, he needed to take Andrew off PAYE (Pay As You Earn) and suggested that he was ready to set up his own consultancy. By this time, Andrew was in his late twenties. He took Don's advice and ran his first business through most of the 1990s, but then in 1998, a company called Future Publishing came to him.

Future Publishing was planning to float on the Stock Exchange and they offered him the job of sales director. The opportunity was too big for Andrew to turn down, so he shut up his business and, as he describes it so wonderfully on LinkedIn, 'turned a disparate group of salespeople into a market-leading professional team'. He says that once again, it was a great learning opportunity as it gave him the chance to practise everything he had been preaching. Future Publishing gained the substantial growth they wanted to float. However, with the dot.com bubble bursting, they had had to downsize and he decided to go off on his own again.

In 2007, Andrew set up Kiss The Fish (KTF for short). It was a rough start with the banks almost closing the company down in 2010 due to the recession and Andrew had to pivot quickly, switching markets away from the big corporations. The business is now thriving.

While 'kiss the fish' was a phrase I had heard, I had no idea where it came from and so I asked Andrew. Kiss the fish is a metaphor for change. He also had a story to tell of its origins. The only other person he found using the name was an American swimming coach. This guy was coaching young kids to swim in a lake where their dads fished for huge catfish. The dads would sit around telling big-fish tales and boasting, and the more they did it, the more terrified the kids would become of swimming in the lake. The coach took a new line, deciding that the kids had to learn to love the fish. And it worked. Andrew says quite apart from being such a great representation of change, the name also suited him as he describes himself as pretty quirky and very much his own person.

Kiss The Fish focuses on helping companies develop their sales and manage change. It works both on strategy and on people to achieve growth. They offer an all-round service – consultancy, training and the supply of part-time sales directors for companies who are growing but don't feel ready for a full-time one of their own, or want someone very experienced to push things forwards fast. Andrew draws on all the experience he has had, working in the UK and internationally, especially in the Pacific Rim and China. He works in a variety of sectors, including tech, packaging, automotive, FMCG (fast-moving consumer goods) and of course, publishing and the media. He has worked with huge names, from Emap, Channel 4 and the Discovery Channel in media to big brands such as Canon, Groupon and SEAT cars, among others. His record in sales is awe-inspiring.

Andrew says he finds that businesses struggle with growth for two main reasons. The first is that they hire the wrong people to sell, by which he means people who 'talk the talk', the type of old-school salesman we both used to work with, who mostly do not have the emotional strength to handle rejection. The second reason is that their sales managers or directors lack strategic experience and process – often they do their own thing, ignoring the company's strategic plan. They only manage day-to-day rather than properly leading, which means they may focus on work effort rather than on the harder improvements in sales quality. Andrew says that they all say they can do the job but don't actually commit and then drift around for six months, by which time the strategic plan has been forgotten about altogether. He is utterly passionate about sales and doing it right. Honesty, he says, is his mantra.

Andrew's definition of personal success: *'Personal success is about happiness – and money is not happiness.'* So, for him, it is to *'love everything you do, look after the family, be a halfway decent human being and have the freedom to do what I want.'*

SALES

When companies come to Andrew for advice on lead solutions, he always tells them to look at how their marketing funnel is working and then come back in six months. The answer more likely lies there. This amazes people who assume he will be biting their hand off for the work and also assume that the problem must lie in sales.

Andrew really hates the poor reputation that sales has. He speaks with passion about how, for example, the big energy and phone companies let consumers pay £20 more than they need to by not telling them there is a better tariff. He is on a personal mission to change this sort of behaviour and have transparency in sales.

Sadly, he says, the sales profession deserves its bad reputation. Its cause is that the average human being is incapable of thinking about anyone else bar themselves. Plus, companies shoot themselves in the foot with the ridiculous. Andrew told me how recently he had been in an Apple franchise (not one of their own stores, he stresses) and he wanted a £900 item. The girl on the desk was lovely and was doing great until he asked her to show him something. She said she couldn't leave her post. He pointed out that he needed to see it to commit to buying, but she was adamant: rules were rules. He didn't buy it.

Andrew thinks that in the past, salespeople have been fraudulent once too often. He always teaches that if you are even halfway honest, you will stand out. People, he points out, do not want to do business with people who only want to take their money. They want to do business with people who help them. He advises that if you want to sell, you have to understand *why* people buy. When he starts working with a company, he always talks to the customers first. Strategy has to be market-led, not invented in someone's brain. The reasons people buy are often very different from why the sales staff and even the business owners themselves think they are. The best place to start is with your current customers, finding out why they buy from you and why they choose your products or services.

It is vital that you understand precisely the benefit to the client of what you are selling – i.e. what problem it solves and how it is going to impact on them for the good. Equally, if you fully understand what value your offering has, then price concerns can go out of the window because the focus is all on value. If you identify why your product is the best, then you don't need to discount it.

Andrew believes that anyone who can communicate well and is prepared to work at it and practise can sell. Irrespective of how much people may wince when first doing it, role play is an essential part of sales training. He believes all new and newish business owners should go out and sell personally, too, because otherwise, they will have nothing to share or teach their sales team later.

'People,' he says, 'don't buy into bullshit like they did in the 80s and 90s. They are too well informed. To sell phenomenally well, you have to focus on the customer completely. That focus has to be both on the person and the business they represent.' Andrew calls this 'customer curiosity' and he bases all his programs on this crucial cultural shift (from selling to buying). 'The seller has to engage the buyer emotionally if he wants to build desire for a product, and if a sales leader can infect his/her team with curiosity, then that leads them to the first base in excellent selling and a great sales culture.'

Emotion is the crucial key in sales and too often, it is missed. Andrew paraphrases the famous quote from the American poet and civil rights activist Maya Angelou, saying that people won't remember what you say, they won't remember what you do, but they will remember how you made them feel. Generating emotion is an absolute fundamental in understanding how to sell. Sincerity and honesty breed trust, so be genuine when you talk to people. Lack of confidence and nervousness can be misconstrued. Lack of consistency in tone or body language can lead to distrust. If you don't believe, nor will they.

Andrew says the key is to forget about yourself, concentrate on the value you are bringing to the other person to meet their needs. It is crucial you have their best interests at heart and that is what comes across. The focus has to be entirely on the customer, not you, and once it is, you forget about any nerves. Salespeople who talk too much are merely focusing on themselves. Andrew also recommends that people try out sales and see if they are comfortable with it, that it is really their thing, instead of selling straight off.

Matrixes are extremely powerful and nailing the numbers is easy if you have an efficient tracking system for your sales and marketing funnel. It is easy to measure, for example, how many calls, on average, it takes to get a lead or a sale. He reminds me of the Tom DeMarco quote, 'You can't control what you don't measure'.

One strategy to make your first contact with people is something you can develop. For example, you can measure what works and what doesn't. This applies to both the mediums you use to approach people and the language you use in your opening lines. Knowing what works also increases your confidence and as your confidence goes up, so too do the sales. Andrew says his best advice is to solve the customer's problem and always keep going. Follow your dream more than a plan. Keep reminding yourself what that dream is. Be prepared to fall sometimes, but go back and get going again.

Key takeaways:

- Find people with the emotional strength to sell and managers with strategic experience;
- Understand why people buy;
- Always be honest when you are selling.

22

Selling Globally
Anneke van den Broek, Rufus & Coco

ANNEKE'S STORY

When Anneke was five, her father taught her to swim, telling her that she should say out loud five times a day, 'I can do anything I want to if I try,' getting louder with each one. He was a big man, 6'4", with a strong Dutch accent, and had played national football for New Zealand after the war. Anneke both feared and admired him. When he died, one of his friends told Anneke she is very like him. The mantra stayed with her for life, but the parental message was mixed. It was a very traditional household – her mother was not allowed to work and continuously budgeted while her dad earned. When Anneke later did an MBA, both spent a month telling her to find herself a man and have children instead. When they saw professional women on the television, they would criticize them.

One day, Anneke overheard her mother regretting the things she had never done and Anneke decided that she wanted a different story for herself. At six years old, she bred mice and sold them to the local pet shop. She also made and sold handicrafts for the local store and artwork that she sold to the neighbours. By 12, she was seeing successful women in suits in magazines and wanted to be one of them.

Her mother gave Anneke her love of animals. Anneke grew up with rabbits, dogs, cats, a turtle she found and a chicken that turned out to be a rooster and had to be given to a nearby farm. You had to beat the dogs to the couch. In her life to date, Anneke has had around 50 pets. She says her school gave her a bum steer, telling her she had to study fashion design to do the fashion marketing she wanted to do. She had been a ballerina and started modelling at 16 and the backstage environment fascinated her. Her talents lie in being creative and, typically, entrepreneurial, at her best with a lot of autonomy. When she did start a business, she was happy to stand behind it, and her then husband helped her to get a business going. Her children now come to work with her sometimes in the holidays or weekends.

Anneke took a master's degree in business administration and a two-year diploma with the Institute of Directors. By 23, she was the marketing manager for 48 David Jones stores across Australia. She had a AU$ 4m spend, one computer in the office shared between four of them and had to organize models, styling and outfits by fax and phone, in addition to dealing with the store managers and sponsors. She says the job taught her a lot about managing people, as did working under three different CEOs there. The female marketing director nudged her to pursue a Master's.

Her next job was working with a board at Australia's largest supplements company, Blackmores. Her dad was a big health nut and had been more likely to use honey on her childhood scrapes and scratches than any over-the-counter cream, so she was already interested in natural remedies. Working for Bonds underwear then gave her experience of internal and external brand alignment as well as the Chinese market. When her next job as general manager for a sportswear company ended in redundancy, she had had enough of corporate politics and this gave her the push she needed to start on her own.

Anneke had seen a gap in the market for natural remedies in pet care. While on holiday in Bali, she drew up a plan on the back of a drinks mat. She came home and put a sign on the door of her second bedroom saying 'World Headquarters', though, at that point, she only planned to be an Asia Pac brand. She had a lot of big ideas.

Anneke told me that at the start, she had held a series of marketing workshops with plenty of red wine and on the second or third occasion, the name Rufus & Coco emerged; better, she felt, than simply 'Anneke's Pet Supplies'.

Starting a business with two children, only 18 months apart, brought its own challenges. Anneke's first labour began while she was packing boxes. She tried, though failed, to bring on the second so she could return in time for an important presentation. She remembers standing in Melbourne airport while still breastfeeding, smartly dressed on the outside, but starting to leak and wondering how she was going to get home.

Anneke remains loyal to the suppliers who bought into her vision in the early days. Initially, selling to Woolworths was a considerable challenge. For three years, they said they would never stock her products as she was too expensive and not 'right' for grocery.

They did trade shows and made mistakes, including telling a potential customer he was unlikely to become a stockist only to discover he was the chairman of Fressnapf,

Europe's largest chain of pet food retailers. Another show in Germany was a catalogue of disasters. Anneke had to borrow a drill to finish making their stand; the wheels came off her suitcase, so 'it was like dragging a dead body;' and half the stand was stolen overnight. She felt like crying, but kept going.

Jen Rogers, the new Woolworths buyer, then appeared and asked why on earth they didn't stock her products. On hearing the story, she set up a meeting. Months later, Anneke remembers standing in Woolworths, one kid balanced on her hip and the other holding her hand, looking at this vast display of products and telling her children that her tears were happy ones.

Another huge challenge was when her distribution company suddenly ended their agreement. By then she was in the throes of divorce and kept hearing her father's voice saying, 'You must always own your own house,' but it was the only collateral she had to invest in the company in order to start their own distribution. In the end, this action brought the company to its customers and also resulted in higher margins, which were needed to sustain the business.

Anneke is extremely witty and had me in stitches, telling me how she couldn't get rid of the taste of their dogs' anti-chewing product for three days. They test everything on humans first. Another story was how she coped when her children were sent home from day-care with headlice. The centre argued with her when she brought them back the next day, but their hair was lice-free: she had used her anti-flea dog shampoo on them.

Anneke is one of Australia's top 50 most powerful women yet she says she still stands at the bottom of their office stairs when she feels low and says to herself,

'Anneke, it's showtime.' She quotes a friend who describes entrepreneurship as 'champagne and razor blade moments'. She takes Coco, her Snowshoe cat, to the office with her in a backpack.

Anneke campaigns for people's rights to be allowed to have their pets with them wherever they are, citing the beneficial mental and physical effects. Their critical mission is to improve humanity one pet at a time.

Anneke's definition of personal success: '*I want to create a legacy and improve humanity a pet at a time. To try and make a difference in the industry. To inspire others to start businesses, especially women. To be my best self and as a mum, support them to be their best selves. For friends to say at my funeral that I lived life with intention and gave it a shot. It is easier said than done and requires self-management and being very mindful.*'

SELLING GLOBALLY

Anneke is aiming to break into 15 countries worldwide and for these to exceed the Australian market. Getting into America was a huge challenge. It cost her enormous amounts of money and her accountant kept telling her to stop trying. They had to step back and take a cautious look at what product to lead with to make it work. I asked Anneke if she would share some advice on how to take your business global and she responded with the following:

'First, do your homework. As a part of our process, each market we look to enter is carefully screened and researched thoroughly. One of the primary resources we use for this is Euromonitor reports, which allow us to identify whether there even is a market for us in the area we are investigating, and then if so, how big that market is. It is then crucial to expand your research to understand any market gaps, the compatibility of your products within the market and retailer interest, as well as to investigate how financial factors such as duties and currency may impact you. With Rufus & Coco, we undertake a full competitor review, as well as a hypothetical feasibility study, to help us determine how realistic our place in that market might be.

'It is also key to really take the time to identify how your target market in this area may be different. It's very likely that due to political, cultural or demographic differences your ideal audience will face slightly different pressure points and may have different needs for products than you are used to. Having all this information ready at your fingertips is crucial to understanding not only if your product will work but also how best to position it in the market for success.

'The next step is to test the waters. Do not be afraid to ask for introductions, which is the fastest way in and around online contact form portals and phone call gatekeepers. We always start by asking our existing contacts if there is anyone they know. Wherever possible, we establish our relationship with new contacts off the back of these introductions.

'In this digital age, tradeshows are still one of the most powerful ways to establish face-to-face relationships and build awareness in the market. They can even provide you with a front-row seat to what your competitors are already doing well.

Many shows have gone digital or semi-digital in order to survive. Maximize your time by conducting informal market research and demonstrating your products in person. Doing this can be the perfect platform for you to test the attractiveness of your offer and receive valuable feedback in real-time. At Rufus & Coco, this is a big part of our "push" strategy. We identify opportunities to present via trade channels like tradeshows or else directly to distributors, sales agents and major retailers before commencing any consumer marketing.

'Next, you need to review your offer. You may find you need to make tweaks in your marketing copy, packaging or product offering to meet both the consumer needs and possibly the legal requirements of the market. For Rufus & Coco, a lot of our packaging is tailored for specific legal, language and retailer requirements. For example, in Australia, it is OK to flush kitty litter down the toilet, with "flushable" used as a key promotional benefit. In California, this goes against state law and so adjustments to the copy were needed. Even things seemingly as simple as the Australian spelling over American spelling or different barcode requirements can require full package redesigns.

'It is also wise to review your proposition. Trying to bring your entire product line into a new market at once can be like trying to open a door with a battering ram. Over the years, we discovered that leading in with our kitty litter offering worked exceptionally well for us as the "pocketknife" that then opened the door up for other possibilities to follow off the back of its success.

'It is also important not to forget intellectual property factors as well and ensure you have secured your logos, names and icon trademarks registrations in key markets. Securing IP can be very expensive, however, so do your research to see if there is any government support. For example, there are a few government grants such as the EMDG (Export Market Development Grant) that you may be eligible for, which can help to support your business in this space.

'The final step is to establish your presence. With over a decade of marketing learnings, we adapt and apply these for each new market but will also sometimes seek to engage with local marketing agencies to assist with building our strategies in the market. Typically starting with a strong focus on digital marketing and instore trade marketing, we also play on our unique "Australian Brand" positioning to secure influencer and PR coverage to get that market talking more about our product and brand.

'It's important to remember that you can have the most amazing digital campaign, but if the product is not well represented or supported at store level, then it's just not going to make an impact. Be prepared for early-morning or late-night conference calls and running online training sessions with retailers to help educate them and support your products' sell-in.

'As we grew, we invested in hiring sales agents who could go door to door educating the stores. They represented us and ensured the staff on the floor were confident in selling our brand so that it might remain top amongst their recommendations. Getting trade marketing right in-store first has always been a key element in our strategy for success. We are then active in entering relevant, local and highly regarded consumer, business and product awards to help us gain recognition and to build up our reputation in that market.'

Key takeaways:

- Do your homework and then test the waters;
- Review your offer and register your IP (intellectual property);
- Establish your presence.

23

Creating a Memorable Customer Journey
James Davidson, tails.com

JAMES'S STORY

When I was starting to put this book together, I went to stay with a very good friend in Suffolk. Her French bulldog, Chini, had been suffering from allergies and when I enquired on her progress, my chum talked ecstatically about how the problems had all cleared up. She told me that she had found this fantastic company online to supply special food and how brilliant the website is, along with the whole customer experience.

I looked up tails.com and saw their customer service scores, loved the website and immediately thought, who better to talk to about how to nail the customer journey, so I contacted James Davidson. James is one of the co-founders of the incredibly successful tailored dog food site, tails.com. The founding team also includes Joe Inglis and Graham Bosher. Between them, they had been involved in some of the leading entrepreneurial companies in the UK. Graham was one of the co-founders of LoveFilm and also founded Graze. Joe, a vet, also had a track record in starting dog food brands. James had worked for Innocent Drinks for many years and has extensive knowledge of how to turn ideas into live products. He ran Innocent's supply chain for many years.

It looked like a combination made in business heaven when they got together in 2013. They took around four months to turn the business model into something they were happy with – they wanted to do everything in-house, feeling they could produce something better that way than if they went down the outsourcing route. The technology was complex, calculating individual pet's nutritional needs and turning it into an especially made food. Age, weight, gender, breed and exercise are all taken into account – dogs have the same nutritional advice needs as we humans do. They assembled a fantastic team of experts, including vets, nutritionists and engineers, to work it all out. Everything looked great. But against all expectations, within a few months of opening, the company was in serious trouble. Graham had raised £5m in seed capital (early stage funding) and they had £3m left, and it felt to some like the right thing to do might be to cut their losses before they lost all their investors' money.

The customers were so disenchanted by the way their subscriptions worked online that a high percentage were not staying subscribed. It cost more to get new customers than they were making from sales. They went to their investors and shareholders. James's pitch and his belief in how they could turn things around won the shareholders' backing to continue and adapt the software so that customers had better visibility and control. I asked James to tell me more of the early challenges they had, as I had read a quote of his in an article: 'Despite our experience, we still deluded ourselves on our genius-ness on the product.' He told me the story as follows:

'Yes, having launched in July 2014 and sold our very first bag of tailored tails.com dry food, we very nearly closed a few months later,' he told me. 'Unfortunately, what we had missed, while we focused so hard to create the very best quality, tailored product, were the real-life needs and expectations of our customers. Thankfully, we realized – not immediately, but very quickly – this mistake and that realization catalyzed us into taking a new approach with the customer at the centre of everything we did. From that point onwards, we have structured the business and our customer journey to take on feedback fast. We are geared to communicate well and make any changes we need to, whether that is changing the feed for our dogs, the delivery times, or to answer any questions that our customers have – rapidly.'

He also shared the learning curve they took from it: 'A handy piece of advice for any new business is to know that although you are deeply passionate about your product, unless you understand and solve the actual (not just theoretical) needs and expectations of your audience, it will not work. It sounds simple, but getting this wrong is potentially the end of the line.'

Everything about tails.com now is customer focused, from the personalized packaging to the fast deliveries, the incredibly user-friendly website to the one-to-one support for each of their customers. James is full of praise for his team, whom he recruits with great care. He says, 'Our Pack [the team] here at tails.com is fundamental to our success. We need and value people with all sorts of specialisms, from our food nutritionists through to our data scientists, engineers and customer service teams.'

Interestingly, he uses people's relationships with failure as one of his benchmarks. He explains, 'How people have responded to failure in the past is one of the things I look for when recruiting new team members: did their failure arise from being courageous and taking risks (which is good) or inaction and being cautious? Were they resilient in the face of it? Did they take personal responsibility for the root cause? And did they learn from their failure and apply that to future action? The answers help to demonstrate if someone has what it takes to make a sustained and positive impact in a high-growth business like tails.com. Especially when we have such a big ambition to change the world of pet food for good.'

The team are encouraged to bring their dogs to work so there are dogs everywhere, which keeps them all focused on what matters. James says his own new puppy, Jasper, is definitely up there in the what-makes-him-happy stakes: 'Some of the most fulfilling and ultimately happy times in my career have been the early – uncertain – days of tails.com when we hustled together as a team, feeling like pioneers, and worked tirelessly to build an entirely new category in the pet food market.' Nevertheless, the tails.com story is one of immense success. In five years, they have grown to have almost 200,000 dogs signed up on tails.com, feeding more than 8 million uniquely tailored meals every month across the UK and France.

James's definition of personal success: *'I do like the Dale Carnegie quote: "Success is getting what you want. Happiness is wanting what you get". I think both are achievable with clarity of purpose, belief in getting there, and, usually, a lot of hard work. As well as that, my top tip is to spend time doing things that you enjoy. To do that with people (or dogs) who make you feel happy. Life is too short to live it otherwise.'*

CUSTOMERS

Without customers, you have no business. No amount of brilliant ideas or flashy technology will make it without that vital ingredient. Everything a company does has to be customer focused. For e-commerce businesses, it is easy to get caught out by focusing on the technology. Undoubtedly, that has to be right. It has to do all the things you need it to do, but more importantly, it must do everything the customers want it to do (including be extremely easy and fast to use). We live in a world where customers want things easily and they want them fast.

For many companies, such as tails.com and Winebuyers (see Chapter 7), the bespoke platforms that perform in hugely complicated ways give them their differential, but it must never be at the expensive of the customer. In addition to user-unfriendly websites, bots are an example of technology that often works against customer relations, causing frustration and anger when they fail to understand our questions. Technology alone, however high tech, is not yet going to create joyful, authentic relationships. Excellent customer service is a lot more than just the website. It is about interacting with the customer at every stage of the journey. You need to excite your customers, to genuinely care for them, and be seen to do so, to give them little extras so the customer journey continually makes them happy. Exceptional customer experience is also about developing trust, and being transparent about who you are and what you do at every stage is vital to attain that.

Delivering excellent customer service starts with establishing what your customer thinks of you (not what *you* think of *you*) and what they want (not what you *think* they want). Never fall into the trap of assuming you know what they think or feel. To do that, you need to talk to them regularly. Ask customers what they want (as James did when things went so wrong), listen and adapt to their feedback. Only by doing so can you even start to anticipate and meet their needs. Once you have a solid understanding of your customers, you can then develop a strategy of what you are aiming to deliver and how you are going to achieve it. That is your customer service strategy. You can then look at the whole customer journey from the moment the customer first comes to you or your website, every step of their journey, through to their buying and your contact post-sale to encourage them to keep buying. You can look for ways to enhance each stage and give pleasure at every step by going the extra mile.

James says that the vital part of delivery lies in having the right people to deliver it. He speaks incredibly highly of his teams and stresses how treating your team right is at the heart of them caring about providing excellent customer service. Great service people do not, for example, slope off at 5 p.m. when a customer needs something urgently, because they have bought into wanting the best for the company's customer.

Your customer service people need to know what they are talking about, too. Thanks to the wealth of information available on the Internet, the customer knows vast amounts about what they want and what is available to them, and they are not going to be impressed if they get to speak to someone who doesn't.

Not everyone makes a great customer service person. They need to be patient, adaptable, able to think on their feet and have that vital ability to empathize and relate to customers. Nothing makes us all angrier than talking to someone who doesn't seem to care at all. They need to be able to apologize and sound as if they mean it and understand why the customer is upset if something has gone wrong. That means they also need to be skilled at listening, not just to the words, but to the tone in which things are said as well, and experts at body language if they are dealing face to face.

People come to do business with you because they are attracted to your brand. Your team has to behave in keeping with the brand otherwise the whole relationship collapses. But equally, they don't want to deal with robots. People are loyal to brands, where real, live people work. Customers buy when they are made to feel good, both by the brand, its values and associations, and particularly by its people.

Customer service must be at the heart of what any company does. It is the keystone to success or failure, as the tails.com journey demonstrates. Getting the customer journey right makes for winning long-term, loyal customers.

Key takeaways:

- However great your product, if the customer experience isn't great then you won't succeed;
- Don't let the technology distract you from the customer;
- Develop an ongoing customer strategy that has talking to your customers at the forefront.

24

Beating the Competition
Sam Kennis, Three Wolves

Sam Kennis grew up in Sydney. He remembers driving past an incredibly busy pub, aged around 16, and thinking, 'What a great way to make money.' When he left school at 18, he went to Alberta in Canada and spent two years there, working in a variety of jobs but mainly gaining bar experience. He then returned to Sydney and went into catering for a time while he studied both business administration and event management at TAFE. He continued to support himself from bar and club work and also while studying, started his first business, supplying waiters for events, from gigs to weddings. A few more years in Canada followed before he decided reluctantly that he ought to study for a degree. The prospect did not hold much appeal, but he finally settled on studying for a degree in media, communication, advertising and marketing distinction at the University of Wollongong. By that point, he was again planning to have his own business, but this time decided he needed some funds behind him so he went to work for Staples, the office supplies company, as a business development executive while continuing to gain experience in bars. He had it in mind to open a bar in Sydney and spent some time researching the market, but concluded the market was saturated and the investment level would be too high.

Through an ex-girlfriend, he met Darren Barber and Grant Buckham, who are both more experienced in business. Darren had the all-round business experience, Sam, the hospitality experience, and Grant a construction background. They discussed the issues Sam had faced with bars in Sydney and Darren suggested that he should visit Cairns, Queensland, where Darren lived, as there was more of a market gap there. Sam flew up and they found a space down an alleyway that they fell in love with and decided it would make a perfect bar venture. It took 10 months from finding the space to opening day, with regular trips from Sydney for Sam and Grant. Darren was living in Cairns and was the guy on the ground for getting the venue set up.

In October 2016, Sam moved to Cairns – it took him three days of continual driving to move up from Sydney. The three formed the Sarrant Group Pty and opened the Three Wolves bar in November 2016. It is a 'laneway' bar, an Australian term originating in the city of Melbourne that roughly translated as 'cool'. It conjures up images of a hard-to-find bar, with cool, savvy customers, innovative cocktails, original art and jazz, a take on the classic speakeasy-style bar. It was the first of its kind in Cairns. They serve food and cocktails, with a heavy emphasis on whisky cocktails.

Sam and Darren hardly drew breath before opening up the tropical Gin Social in the Hilton Hotel in Cairns, closely followed by the Flamingo Tiki bar, the only proper tiki bar, north of Brisbane. A tiki bar is a bar with an exotic, tropical theme specializing in rum-based cocktails. Again, they concentrated on finding the right space, setting up their rum bar right on the esplanade in Cairns.

Meanwhile, Grant remained in Sydney. Then, in 2018, the three were having a beer at a marina in Gosford, down in New South Wales, when they came up with the idea of opening a brewery there and calling it Bay Road Brewery, on the simple basis that they were on Bay Road and the setting was perfect. They opened this at roughly the same time as the Tiki Bar.

Grant has a passion for beer. The micro-brewery is also making a name for itself, focusing on crafting exceptional beer. The space stands out, being light and open and bearing little resemblance to Three Wolves. It is not just a brewery but also a place where the local community comes to eat, drink and hold events. Grant runs all the day-to-day and event side of Bay Road and was the on-the-ground person to get it up and running.

Up in Cairns, Sam and Darren spotted another unusual building on the market that appealed to them, bang opposite the original Three Wolves bar. Built in 1905, rare for the modern city of Cairns, it was an old stable block and they could instantly see its potential, although they were unsure precisely what to do with it. The plan had been to find premises for another bar, but they could see two issues. Even in the short space of time since they had started, more and more bars had opened in Cairns and the market was getting saturated. Also, opening another bar opposite their already successful bar did not make sense.

They came up with the idea of a gin distillery. Unlike whisky, gin is fast to brew, taking only 36 hours from start to finish, so it was the perfect product for tropical distilling. They renovated the building, realizing that the open space would also make an ideal venue in the same way as Bay Road worked. They would be able to invite their clients in for training and tasting sessions and hold master-classes. They laid it out to have a tasting bar, space for tables and chairs, and retail space.

Wolf Lane Distillery, which is a micro gin distillery producing Wolf Lane Gin, opened in November 2019. Despite being so new on the market, their tropical gin has already won the gold medal at the Australian Gin Awards and received a great deal of notice after being placed fourth in the Australian Top 100 Gins of 2019. Wolf Lane Navy Strength Gin has since been named the world's best at The Gin Guide Awards 2020 and also won the Best in Australasia trophy at the awards.

Worldwide, hospitality was badly hit by the pandemic of 2020. The Wolves adapted fast. Their distillery was one of the first in Australia to produce a World Health Organization-approved hand sanitizer. They also brought forward another plan they had and launched Cocktails Online, through which they sell ready-made cocktails across Australia. They had always planned to expand and this was another way to do so, along with plans to produce vodka and liqueurs and wanting to take their labels global.

Sam's definition of personal success: '*To be happy with what I am doing. That isn't the amount of money I make or how many venues we have, but it's about delivering a product people love. That is what we are all about: beautiful venues and products people love.*'

STAYING AHEAD OF THE COMPETITION

When I first asked Sam how they approached this, he said their viewpoint is that competition is both good and healthy. He says that they make a point of working with the competition, sending customers to other bars when they are looking for a particular drink or style of food and getting the same in return from them. They believe it is necessary to be aware of the competition, but not worry about it. If you overthink it, you will never get started on plans. It is most important not to let it get in the way of what you are doing and what you are passionate about, and not be over-governed by trends. This thinking struck me as being very much in keeping with a piece of advice I had read from Darren Barber, who said that in business generally, you should not overthink it, but just do it.

Sam says he sums his approach up to beating the competition as the three Cs. First, there is the concept, a great idea, and having clarity about what it is you are doing. Then you need confidence both in yourself and what you are doing. Finally, there is the commitment, that essential ingredient for every business.

When you look at both sides of their businesses, it is clear how this pans out. Sam had a clear vision of the type of bar he wanted, a kind that existed in Sydney and had not yet reached Cairns. The first Three Wolves bar is a perfect fit for that concept in style. They spent considerable time planning the interiors to maximize the beauty of the space and fit the themes to compliment that. With the tiki bar, they jumped right on the craze they saw sweeping across Australia. Unlike average bars, they want every visit to be an experience that stands out in people's minds, experiences being on point with the market right now.

When opening new bars, their strategy is always to look at what is missing in the town. The market is one they know well. The bars that have followed have been deliberately niche, filling gaps they see that the other bars are not. By the time they opened Flamingos, they were aware of how the market was filling up, so they also kept it small enough to remain healthy with small numbers.

The experience concept is applied to what they serve and how they serve it, too. The Three Wolves bar features whisky and cocktails, but these have been devised with great care to make them personalized and unobtainable elsewhere. The sugar used in the cocktails, for example, is the local sugar cane that predominates in the area. However, it is also down to procedures, which Sam believes is the secret to scaling up. He points out that a pilot and co-pilot who have never worked together before can still jump on any plane and work seamlessly together. This is down to training and procedures. Having those procedures in place also allows him to step away once the venue is up and running:

'Everything needs to be done the same way by any individual. The idea is to be able to bring anyone from the street and they should in theory be able to open and close a bar. Not saying we employ just anyone. We look for personality, loyalty and a willingness to learn. Making cocktails can be taught, but customer service and love for hospitality you can't teach. Staff are the backbone of every business. Treat them right and they will treat you correctly.'

Their customer reviews are outstanding, with a heavy emphasis on the atmosphere and warmth of service. To achieve that has been one of the battles and Sam says they would not have done it without a great team. Traditionally, staff turnover is high with Cairns being a transitional city. You have to concentrate on looking after your team exceptionally well to encourage them to stay. He advises that you should look to surround yourself with people who are stronger than you are and as committed as you are.

Sam says they did a great deal of research before starting, but despite the volume of work and Darren's experience, they still missed things. They begin with their own concepts but are open to listening to their customers and continually evolving, renovating, improving, putting on different events.

With the distillery and the brewery, they again study how to stand out from the competition. Down at Bay Road, Grant carries out research and development of his recipes and works through exactly how they are going to differentiate from other breweries. There are over 160 gin distilleries in Australia so they had to make the taste of their gin just as distinctive. They had always wanted the distillery to support the local community, so they drew on this to devise a Tropical Gin, picking up the north Queensland flavours for which Sam had found no near competition. To support the local community, they buy the botanicals for the gins from small farmsteads in the neighbouring Tablelands.

Within months, the gin was winning awards. Sam says these are great, not so much for bringing sales directly, but because they are an affirmation of your place against the competition. That makes the product immediately easier to sell and to stand head and shoulders above the rest. He believes that competition is both the best and worst thing about hospitality: 'The more venues in an area, the more people come out and do bar crawls, experience nights out and enjoy hospitality. If there are more places to check out, people come, have one drink and move on. If only a few venues are in the area, the venue will be packed and flooded. This also can be tough because people will get bored if nothing new is happening.

'I always look at what the local competition is doing and ask myself how they are doing it, how well they are really doing, what their busiest times are, discover why they are busy if we are not. You always need to watch what competition are doing, but don't allow yourself to be worried by it, or to feel the need to do something similar. People love variety and doing something different. Imagine a world where all the restaurants and bars do the same thing … boring! Stick to what you know. Do what you know best and be confident in your concept.'

Key takeaways:

- Don't let the competition overwhelm you – stick to what you do best;
- Look for the market needs the competition isn't fulfilling;
- Have a great concept, confidence, commitment.

25

Protecting Your Digital Reputation
Simon Wadsworth, Igniyte Ltd

Simon Wadsworth's first business, the award-winning Internet design agency Brand New Media, was established back in 1994. He had graduated from Bradford University and gone to work for the European Commission as an IT and telecoms consultant. While on holiday, he visited a friend who was at university in the US. The drawback to the trip for Simon was that he was unable to find the latest results for his much-loved football team, Manchester City. His friend told him to wait there, printed off the results and explained: 'This is the Internet.' For Simon, it was a light-bulb moment and prompted him to leave the European Commission to set up an Internet company and become an early UK pioneer in the industry.

Simon was one of the first to advise companies on how the then-emerging Internet would change everything. Businesses caught on fast and by 2000, he had household names, including Heinz, Procter & Gamble and Tesco, among his extensive portfolio of clients. He sold Brand New Media, but 18 months later, set up a new agency, Swamp, which became one of the most well-known digital agencies in the UK, with another broad repertoire of household brands on its books. Swamp was also recognized for its contribution to the growing recognition of Leeds as a serious place to do business.

In 2006, Simon sold Swamp, going on to form Igniyte, a specialized online reputation management consultancy, in 2009. He says that for him, the most exciting part of a business cycle is the first year when you are setting up something new. When you are testing out what you can and can't do, it can become addictive and this is at the core of what drives him to set up new businesses.

Igniyte was initially a digital marketing agency, but Simon was always at the forefront of business trends and that soon changed. One of his clients came to him for specific help on recovering their position on Google searches. Within nine months, he'd changed the focus of Igniyte to an online reputation management company after recognizing the need and potential for online reputation specialists. Ten years on and Igniyte is a leading authority on online reputation management, with clients around the world.

At Igniyte, the team of specialists are passionate about ensuring people, brands and businesses are all treated fairly online. They help repair, build and grow online reputations, using tried-and-tested specialist tactics, SEO (search engine optimization), content, PR, social media and online review management. All of this is a crucial element of contemporary business. People come to Igniyte after receiving the poor reviews, negative press stories and personal attacks online that they are out of their depth to deal with. Inevitably, they need some guidance as well. The effects on people when attacked online can be devastating – Igniyte works to restore balance.

Every case is different. Simon says he is asked a lot about removing different types of content, from dated press articles to damaging images and videos. He also tells how they have had letters and calls from individuals from all walks of life, asking about the 'right to be forgotten'. Now recognized as a leading authority in online reputation management and digital marketing, Simon writes extensively for international, national and specialist press and broadcast media. He is a published author, with his book *The Captains Club: The Men Who Led United* and has a blog at www.reputations.org.uk. He kindly explained to me exactly why this is so important.

Simon's definition of personal success: He says it is multi-layered. The thing he is most proud of is his kids. On top of this, for him personal success ultimately includes aiming for a mix of enjoying his work, creating something that has real value, making his company a place that people want to work and grow in, and making it famous and profitable.

ONLINE REPUTATION MANAGEMENT

Negative results on Google page one are a worry for businesses and individuals as this can heavily impact their reputation – how people perceive them and whether they choose to do business with them or not. Simon gave me the following stats:

- One in five companies are unhappy with how they are portrayed on Google page one;
- One in three companies say negative content has damaged their business;

- Forty-six per cent of companies have been or are worried about negative press coverage;
- Companies risk losing 22 per cent of business with one negative on the first page of their search results – and 70 per cent of potential customers with four or more negatives;
- Executives say on average, 49 per cent of the reputation of their company is attributable to their CEO's reputation.

He explained further: 'We've all seen plenty of personal and business reputation crises play out on social media and other online outlets. From easyJet's Twitter blunder [when a link to their privacy statement had missed out one letter and mistakenly directed clients to a porn site instead] to Roseanne Barr's tweets citing *Planet of the Apes* when criticizing former President Barack Obama's aide, Valerie Jarrett. And the fallout from Forever 21 sending out diet bars with online orders of plus-size clothing. That is just a few examples. Although the initial social media storm is short-lived, the impact that these events have on search results can be far-reaching – both for the business involved and the individual.

'At their worst, these incidents will ruin an individual or business. But they can also result in an influx of #boycott hashtags, a ruined reputation, lost revenue and a lack of future opportunities. In this social media age, there is no escaping the backlash when it comes to a very public business or personal reputation crisis – prevention is always better than cure.'

Simon explained that social media scandal will stay around forever. Unfortunately, the adage of 'what happens in Vegas, stays in Vegas' no longer exists. The Internet is a permanent place. And even after years and years of being online, some will still forget that hitting that post, share or like button will mean it is there forever.

Simon gives the example of Shane Gills from *Saturday Night Live*, who was fired from his role as a cast member on the show when old videos surfaced showing him making racist slurs. Realizing your mistake and deleting the post, fast, won't always save you as some followers may have taken a screenshot and published it in some way.

Simon has been kind enough to share the following advice on how to avoid a personal crisis and how to survive one:

- Risk assess your own online content. Ask yourself, whenever you post something, 'Will this impact me in five years?' Start by going through your Instagram and Twitter feed, as well as your Facebook timeline and any other social media platforms you use. And don't forget to include blogs, guest publications or anything where you might appear online. If you find any problems, start cleaning up your digital past. We now live in a world where people will actively dig for negative posts, so it pays dividends to do this.
- Check your language. Using foul language is fine if that is your tone of voice and part of your personal brand, but if you're associated with someone else or are a representative for a company, or might even have the opportunity to work with another brand in the future, it's not a good idea. Every business or brand tends to keep its language 'PC' and will only work with an individual or brand that won't impact directly on those brand values. Some great brands use

swearing well (Dollar Shave Club and Thug Kitchen, I'm looking at you), but in the interests of avoiding a personal brand crisis, let's stay away from swearing.

- Ask yourself, 'What would my mother say if she read this?' It's always a practical way to approach anything on social media with caution. Unless your personal brand is to be outrageous, if you want to post something that might be slightly risky, consider how something you write online would be seen by your nearest and dearest. If 'Aunt Susan' wouldn't appreciate the meme, joke, comment about a competitor, then there is always a good chance that your fans, clients, stakeholders or customers wouldn't like it either – 'It's nice to be nice'.

- Stay away from politics. Unless you're involved in politics directly, it's just better to avoid commenting. You can easily offend followers who will never share the same opinions as you. As always, there are exceptions to the rule. Anything that supports equality, such as LGBTQ rights, or movements like #MeToo or Black Lives Matter, is always seen as favourable on social media – when genuine. Ethics matter.

- Be prepared. A personal or business reputation crisis can strike without warning so having a solid plan personally or a business reputation management crisis plan in place is essential. Knowing who you will work with if something happens can make all the difference. Research by law firm Freshfields Bruckhaus Deringer shows that a quarter of crises spread to international media within an hour, while companies take an average of 21 hours to respond.

- No one is immune from a social media scandal, whether it is something in your business or personal life. The most important thing is to **ACT – Assess. Control. Transform.**

Assess the damage. Ascertain sentiment, capture data and monitor the harm so you can leverage the insights to strategize.

Think about how much control you have over which channels and what you can do to influence each one. Create a plan of action to put you back in **Control**.

A well-thought-out strategy will fix and **Transform** your reputation online. It is time to start planning what you need to do.

Simon adds: 'When a business or personal reputation crisis hits, it can be unfair and devastating. Your hard-earned reputation matters to you and it matters to the experts at Igniyte, too. You'll need an immediate short-term plan to deal with it and a long-term strategy to rebuild your reputation.'

Key takeaways:

- Online reputation and Google page one results are now critical to business;
- Prevention is better than cure so always be prepared and plan for the worst;
- ACT on a social media strategy.

PART SIX

Cash, Value and Your Future

Another mistake I made (and I have barely scratched the surface with the ones I have mentioned so far) was to assume that growth is golden. It isn't. Scaling too quickly is an easy way to put yourself out of business. It certainly isn't a guarantee of higher profits.

In my joyous naivety, I assumed that if we sold £1 million worth of furniture and got, for the sake of argument, 10 per cent profit, then when we sold £2 million, it would automatically mean we still got 10 per cent profit. I could not have been more wrong. Because we failed to nail how we were growing in nearly every way, what had been a pretty yummy profit that would have kept the core team and me very happily turned into a torrent of lost cash. Of course, it isn't as simple as that. Businesses can't stay still and we wouldn't have been able to survive without investing some of those profits, but it would have been less stressful and more profitable to keep small and beautiful.

We had to use invoice financing for cash flow and a chunk of every bit of revenue never reaching your bank is always going to hurt. Here, Lex Deak discusses why cash flow is so vital, how to sustain it to profit better and how to understand what makes a company have value. Ramping up the profit as you grow is an art. Mike Lander has built several businesses and knows precisely how to achieve it and shares several key points. So has Jeff Fenster and here, he explains one of his key strategies of vertical integration.

Serial pharma entrepreneur Natalie Douglas, with successes on both sides of the pond, both as a founder and a CEO, explains when it is right to move between the two and when you should consider moving on. This is a great lesson. I was anxious to work on the business rather than in it as that was what I had been told and Natalie explains why that is not always a good thing.

Then there is the thorny question of considering a sale. To achieve a serious sum when selling, you need to scale further still. However, that doesn't mean you don't want to both add to your bottom-line value and have an option to sell, should some reason arise that you want to. Ignorance of selling a business was one of my most dangerous disadvantages. It left me open to some truly atrocious advice from several predatory people. Jeremy Harbour explains how to add to the value of your business and how to be sale-ready – just in case.

26

Understanding Your Company's Value
Lex Deak, KinderList

LEX'S STORY

Lex Deak's fascination with technology was born early by breaking a computer and putting it back together. The process of elimination, of finding out which bit did what and went where, had him hooked. He taught himself about hardware and software. He had a passion for the *Back to the Future* films – Doc Brown, in particular – and wanted to be an inventor.

When he won a bursary to the prestigious private Merchant Taylors' School, Lex saw serious wealth for the first time. So, at 11, he started buying electronics, from pagers to mini-disc players, and selling them to his classmates. His widowed mum had built up an all-female cab company to a million-pound turnover and Lex spent much of his time in the office, soaking up business. He grew up unaware of business risks.

Lex went to Manchester to study for a BA in management and started Profile Design, importing modern and repro furniture from China and India. His next venture was an eBay drop-off shop called Sell it, Shack. When he sold this to Auctioning4u, he went to Marrakech to celebrate. A new holiday destination at that time, it was dubbed 'the nearest you can go to get far away'. Lex and his mum browsed local estate agents' windows and made 'back-of-a-fag-packet' calculations on how much buying an old riad would be versus the price of a hotel room. Lex suddenly found himself the owner of a run-down riad. He converted it to a luxury boutique hotel and sold it on.

Lex then started FamilyFridge, an online social network for families. He took the business to the BBC TV series *Dragons' Den* and won investment from Dragon Julie Meyer. After the first week of elation had worn off, he was in for a grim awakening. According to Lex, Meyer moved him into offices next door to hers, but whenever Lex tried to talk about the deal, there was always something else she needed to see and several weeks until she could look at each answer. This prevarication dragged on for a year. Lex knew if he looked for funding elsewhere, people would assume something was wrong with the business if Meyer hadn't gone ahead, and gave up on his dream. Later, Meyer's firm ACL was put into administration and investigated by the City regulator over allegations of mismanagement and misuse of investor funds.

By chance, Lex was approached about a job at The Supper Club, a membership club for high-growth business founders, which is where we met. The year there gave him time to take stock, grow his network and develop. He started The Investment Club for its members, which still runs successfully today.

In 2014, he founded QVentures, a members-only investment club. He partnered with Quintessentially, the global private members club and concierge service. QVentures is the most successful Angel network in the UK, within around £130m of investment deals. Soon, QVentures had itself broken the £1m turnover, building equity value from the shares they took. Its rapid success came in part from Lex's skill in signing up 20 high-profile people early. Founders of Moonpig, Airmiles, Innocent and Skyscanner were among those who had additional perks in return for the credibility of their names in the publicity.

Lex's next company was Tendr, a Tinder-style app that was an aggregator for crowdfunding. After great publicity, thousands of investors downloaded it, but Lex says that sadly, there was no robust commercial model under it. They also received a cease and desist order on the name. Lex raised capital and relaunched as OFF3R. It did start to generate an income, but being an affiliate network in financial services proved both time-and money-consuming. Lex raised more funding and regrouped again, this time as Pia (personal investment assistant), with an impressive board behind him. But eventually, the technology needed proved just too expensive and so he reached the difficult decision to stop while they were still able to ensure everyone was paid.

It was a doubly challenging time as Lex had also lost a great deal of personal money in currency trading and felt like he was in a downward spiral. He says that the currency deal was a hard lesson that anything worth having takes hard work and dedication. As he emerged from the shadows, an old idea resurfaced and defined as KinderList, an online store for children's gifts and experiences. Lex launched this with his wife, though she has now returned to her career in the media world. Having become a parent himself, Lex says he loves being in a world of colour, fun and laughter. The timing was perfect, hitting the dramatic change to all-online caused by Covid-19. There are elements in the tech that could scale into other industries, so he is feeling bullish about the future.

Lex's definition of personal success: It *'evolves all the time'* as he gets older. *'Now it is to adapt the Buddhist philosophy of letting go of desire. Wanting things takes all the enjoyment out of having and experiencing them. As soon as you have them, you want something else. If you can let go of the wanting, you will be able to enjoy the present.'*

UNDERSTANDING YOUR COMPANY'S VALUE

While many of us drift, as I myself did, into scaling up, believing it must be the right thing to do, others are on a mission to grow further with capital investment or to sell. With experience on both sides of the funding table, Lex seemed a great person to talk to about this.

We started by discussing the oft-heard statement, 'cash is king'. Lex interprets this as the view that profit-making or robust businesses are king. He had heard one of the Dragons complain that cash was king when the company pitching had stock to the value they needed. Lex feels it is stating the obvious. And of course, having no money, you will feel like a pauper.

Cash being king often comes up in relation to to cash flow. Lex thinks this comes down to simple common sense.

If you are a company that is struggling to survive, as so many have in recent times, then cash being king is about common sense. Healthy cash flow then means stripping back the unnecessary, shortening your invoices and payment terms, cutting back excess overheads and negotiating longer payment terms with your suppliers if that is relevant to your business.

But cash being king can mean something completely different in another sector. Lex gives the example of tech businesses Uber, Monzo and Revolut, none of which are profitable but which private equity, venture capital and sovereign wealth funds will nevertheless keep backing. The investment is worth it: once these companies reach a critical mass of customers, they become a monster and a massive profit centre. For companies like these, cash is king to the extent that they need it to grow super-normally quickly and for a land grab, paying over the odds for significant scale customer acquisition. In technology, it is usual for revenues to lag and then investment becomes essential.

'Cash is king' therefore means different things in different sectors, just as funding is available on various metrics. An industry with barriers to scale won't be able to access capital until they are at least near to profitability. Another sector would simply require you to show a successful model that would work at scale.

Lex says that the steps he would advise when prepping to look for investment form an exercise that should be done regularly within your business even if you are not seeking financing. Going through these steps helps you understand what your company is like and what your ambitions are. It will also make you better equipped to understand your business and ready it for fundraising or exit. Either situation can sneak up on you, an opportunity for growth, running out of cash or an unexpected reason to sell. Trying to do either at the last minute could be a disaster – as Lex says, there is nothing so obvious as a desperate founder who needs cash. You can smell it a mile off. You can't afford to wait until three months before you need the money, you would be sweating over how you pay the staff and it would show.

Lex suggests chunking the preparation activity into distinct work groups. You should start by getting your collateral together. Many entrepreneurs begin by having conversations with potential investors very early on, before they have their ducks lined up. They approach potential buyers too soon, too. Instead, they should be forming a bulletproof plan and working out exact figures rather than drifting into soft conversations in the hope that someone is going to say, 'Oh, I love the idea, here's loads of money, don't worry about the detail, you just go and crack on.'

The reality is that putting together a deal, a compelling deck, takes time, as does registering shares for the Enterprise Investment Scheme (EIS) or the equivalent in whichever country you are in, if you intend to go this route. If you have that conversation too early, any deal will go cold by the time you are ready. Lex says that investors like a time limit and the scarcity feeling. So as part of your internal exercise, you should put together your pitch deck and practise it on friends and family. You want to test if the message and structure are right – and you will start to see your company and its value with outside eyes.

Prepping should ideally be done about nine months in advance and constant readiness will mean you are into the process. For investment, there is a sweet spot in the time frame to apply. This spot is when you have demonstrated a market fit and have enough figures and customer data that you can extrapolate that into a model that an investor can understand. You need to reduce it to show that if they put *x* in, it will mean they get *y* out. Always remember that the value they will get out may not relate entirely to profit.

Do your research on the people you are approaching. If you go to a crowdfunding platform with a deal that is more of a private equity (PE) deal or vice versa, you will receive a rejection, however good it is. Get to fewer people and quicker and follow it up in a way that acknowledges this as the most critical sales exercise of your life.

When putting together the deal, there are useful platforms such as SeedLegals, that are very easy to understand. You want to ensure that your terms are unequivocal, easy to understand and actionable. Then you need to demonstrate that the market really likes what you are doing. This may show in turnover, but depending on the sector, it might be in other ways. Lex explains that they took KinderList to The Baby Show at ExCeL London. With a tiny stand costing £1,500, a total of £100,000 worth of items was added to the wish list. While it wasn't firm orders, it still demonstrated their ability to capture a significant market intent. These figures can form a part of showing how well you are doing and how much the market likes you, which in turn will increase your value.

At an exit stage, the value of your company should be self-evident. The spread of your customers and the risk in that spread affects value. Other factors, in addition to users and market traction, will depend on the sector. These could include the value of any IP and other assets, how long it would take someone else to get to your point in the market and if you have something that no one else has or exclusive contracts with healthy amounts of time left on them.

The classic metric for exits is EBIT (earnings before interest and taxes), a formula calculated by subtracting the cost of goods sold and operating expenses from total revenue). Still, particularly in tech, you see valuations that deviate significantly from that. However, you should bear EBIT in mind. A continual focus on all these figures will make you aware of your company's value.

Equally, from day one, you should run and structure your business as if a sale were just around the corner, whatever your plans. It is a real discipline and good practice that will make any exit or investment conversations more fluid and avoids last-minute panic.

There are many pitfalls in exits. Taking stock in the acquiring firm can go horribly wrong if the company tanks. Onerous earn-out periods with a lot of warranties and restrictions and impossible-to-meet KPIs (key performance indicators) can leave with you with very little. A deal that drags out until it's 90 per cent complete and then collapses can completely exhaust an entrepreneur to the point where their lack of focus leaves the business on its knees. Investors know this and some use it as a deliberate negotiating tactic.

Lex says one trick he learned at the Supper Club is to go and have a holiday before negotiating for investment or exit. You will then appear bronzed and relaxed when it comes to the negotiations. How you come across is critically important.

Key takeaways:

- Cash and profitability are viewed differently in different sectors;
- Testing the value of your company will enhance the way you run it;
- Understanding value makes investment and sales easier and quicker.

27

Scaling Up to £1m Profit

Mike Lander, Piscari

MIKE'S STORY

I had met Mike Lander a few times at business dinners and was intrigued to hear how he has achieved his considerable success. Fascinatingly, he told me that everyone in his family was a corporate worker and so growing up he had no idea entrepreneurs even existed. Instead, he started his career in an engineering firm in the north-west of England.

In his mid-20s, he saw a BBC TV programme called *Troubleshooter* with Sir John Harvey-Jones. It was to light a spark in Mike that has stayed with him throughout his career as he's built his own companies and helped others. Perhaps it is not surprising that the first company he acquired was a consultancy, he says.

During the first half of his career, from 1980 to 2002, Mike worked for large corporations, where he learned his craft and management discipline. Since 2002, he has been freelancing, building entrepreneurial businesses and providing SME advisory services. He says he took all of the good stuff from big-company disciplines and flexed them into the needs of small, entrepreneurial businesses, enabling them to scale. He believes that he achieved this challenging transition by being adaptable, curious and continually learning.

Mike described his first step out of the corporate world and into what he thought of as building his own business in 2002, a consultancy business called Vision2Execute. He had 20 years of experience and aimed to help companies who struggled to turn a vision into an implementation programme that delivered results.

An early client, a director of a global healthcare company, gave him some very blunt advice. He told Mike that he was trying to offer a bit of everything and while it all sounded great, he, as a client, was left with no idea of what Mike's primary offering was. Mike was shocked. He says he had naively believed that he could do anything the client wanted whereas, in reality, large companies buy very specific skills from micro-SMEs. He advises any new/growth business to develop a ruthless focus and niche expertise before broadening any offering.

Mike spent four years providing this service as a freelancer rather than building a company and learned the differential between selling himself and building a business. He was still planning the latter, patiently building a small war chest of savings in preparation for when the right opportunity arrived. Mike advises people to either have that pot built up or keep a side hustle going to provide some income in case of failure. He doesn't believe in chance, but in preparation, perseverance and continually evaluating opportunities.

In 2006, Mike acquired Piscari and CSL, an education consultancy that grew from £10m to £20m revenue. He had realized that the quickest way to scale was to buy an existing company. People said he was crazy to buy CSL, but he proved them wrong. Look for somewhere that you can see there is headroom to grow and opportunities to improve margins, he advises.

Mike says he learned a great deal, including that you should not diversify into businesses that you don't understand. He learned never to 'bet the farm' as this could destroy all the value you have created. Never over-leverage with debt as lenders won't flinch at taking your business away from you if you are in trouble. He came to understand how critical it is to find highly talented people with the right attitudes and integrity, which is a reminder of why VCs tend to invest in great people, not just great business plans.

Together with a partner, Mike also started Profitflo, in 2011. Profitflo was a procurement consultancy working with private equity-backed entrepreneurial firms to drive sustainable EBITDA improvement through procurement. Your EBITDA is the company's net earnings with tax, interest, depreciation and amortization factored in. He rapidly discovered how to see things through an investor's lens, which was very different from working solely with owner/operators. Mike advises that where possible, becoming a buyer before you sell is a great learning curve to understanding win-win deals through a customer's eyes.

Mike also started Ensoul, an architectural design business. There, he discovered that, unlike with corporate budgets, every penny is measured when you are spending an individual's hard-earned cash. Since 2017, Mike has also been an SME board advisor, challenging entrepreneurs to grow. He says you should never underestimate the value your knowledge has to others when communicated and packaged correctly.

When Mike sold the school's business in 2016, he retained the name Piscari and this brand now helps small companies to negotiate better deals with procurement professionals in big companies. Here, he says he has seen how hard it is to find talent with proven strategic and tactical customer acquisition digital marketing skills, which are crucial to building businesses online.

Mike believes in giving back. He and his wife set up the Piscari Trust to support young people from disadvantaged backgrounds and help them to get into meaningful work. Mike was also a non-executive director (NED) for the NHS Institute for Innovation and Improvement. He saw what an amazing job the NHS does with limited resources, but like any highly complex/political organization (public or private), driving through lasting change takes time, patience and a desire to learn. NEDs can play three vital roles in public sector bodies: external perspective/challenge, enhanced commercial acumen and pace.

Mike says he is fortunate to have a family that understands his working patterns and flexible clients in terms of when/how they engage with him. He has designed his life so that he sees his wife and son a lot in the week, albeit his days get stretched.

Mike's definition of personal success: *'A loving and happy family with enough money to enjoy life (forever). To help other entrepreneurs achieve the success they desire. To always be learning.'*

SCALING UP TO £1M PROFIT

I asked Mike if he would share his expertise on why companies struggle to scale up and what they should be doing. I am enormously grateful for his generosity in providing the advice set out here.

Mike says he gets given many reasons for people's failures to scale up: 'It was just too competitive, or we were just unlucky, and it was bad timing. We never wanted to achieve £1m revenue in the first place. I knew what to do, but my team just didn't get it. We tried loads of things, but none of them really worked.' The truth is always in a mix of factors, he adds. If it were simple to attain success, everyone would do it and be wealthy. In his experience, there are seven main reasons, the first of which is timing. Timing means working out the right time to enter and exit a market – it has nothing to do with luck.

Most entrepreneurs start businesses with people they know and you certainly need people you can trust on the crazy journey. However, it is critical to add people who have the right skills and know exactly what they are doing, as well as trusted friends.

Time, money and people are always in short supply. You need to ignore all distractions and focus on your core proposition/market. The greater the focus, the greater the traction. There is a caveat in that, to discover what that core is early, you need to 'do a little and learn a lot' – fast. He approaches it by finding and researching niches in markets where you can solve tangible problems and create 10x value for customers. From there, you can build out a proposition that you can start to test on clients.

Mike says this adage that you need to work on, not in the business, is entirely true. You continue coaching your people on solving complex issues and contributing, but spending all your time doing these is not going to get you to £1m revenue growth. Check how you split your time on the two.

Business plans are necessary, but without the feedback from potential customers, you will never know if you have nailed what you are offering at the right price and with the right benefits. Scale-up will not be achieved without a compelling, market-tested proposition. Once in the whirlwind, people all too easily forget to maintain focus on consistent, high-quality delivery to clients. This delivery creates a buzz about your company and leads to the necessary word-of-mouth marketing and referrals.

Finally, he warns, while learning, evolving and feedback are all essential to forming a sound business proposition, always beware of flogging a dead horse. You need an open mind and to take account of feedback from people you respect. Some people look for a perfect answer that will magically ensure their business scales up fast and well. The reality is there is no such thing; it is a combination of factors.

Procurement advice appears regularly in Mike's career, yet he observes wryly that most entrepreneurs glaze over at its mere mention. He explained how important it is to scaling-up. Firstly, there is cost control: 'In its raw form, procurement is a discipline that drives cost out of the business, sustainably. As one of my clients described it, "When procurement is done well, it's the gift that keeps on giving." Then there is sales conversion: if you understand how procurement professionals work and what motivates them, then you will understand how to negotiate with them when you come to sell bigger deals to bigger clients.'

I was keen to hear Mike's advice on the right steps to take when scaling up. He points out that every business is at a different stage of evolution, so a true step-by-step guide is never possible, but some common foundations must be in place to start the journey:

- Leadership: A strong, clear, visionary CEO/MD who people can follow, plus a small number of extremely talented direct reports that can make it happen.
- Strategy: If you (and your teams) don't know where you're going, then any path will get you there!
- Financial management and KPIs: It's a lasting truth that businesses don't fail because of weak profitability, they fail because of poor cash-flow management. You will need a Dashboard system with Lead and Lag indicators (financial and non-financial performance indicators used in project management) so that you will know in advance if you are on track as you scale up.
- Sales and account management: You need a sales and marketing engine/system, not just one talented individual with a spreadsheet.
- Operational systems and processes: To scale any business, you need repeatable ways of doing, monitoring and managing the way value is delivered to your clients.
- Focus: It doesn't need explaining. You either are, or you aren't, focused and it makes a huge difference to success.
- Accountability: You need an organizational design that is scalable, with clear lines of accountability (so people know what they own), a recruitment process and reward mechanisms.

Key takeaways:

- You need the right leadership team;
- You need the right operational and reporting systems;
- You need massive amounts of focus, too.

28

When to Move Up or On

*Natalie Douglas: Lucidity LLC,
RareiTi, Inc*

Natalie Douglas is a serial health tech entrepreneur and investor, successful in both the UK and US, and has worked her way up the hard way. She was born in Poole, Dorset. Most of her family ran small, local businesses. She describes herself as a quite naive, country girl with a passion for reading and outdoor life. Science did not inspire her and she says that she wouldn't have known what a pharma company was, but a part of her wanted to travel and see how far she could go in life.

In due course, she moved away and was working in marketing when by chance, a friend in recruitment asked a favour. The chum needed to keep an occupational health client happy and had no one for them to interview. She asked Natalie to go until she could find a real applicant. To everyone's surprise, Natalie accepted their subsequent offer and took her first step into healthcare. From there, she applied for a rep's job with Johnson & Johnson. The intensive training programme was a struggle, with her O-level biology no match for the others' biochemistry degrees. Presenting made her feel sick with nerves.

Determinedly, she became a top-performing rep. Her inability to be too scientific became her strength as she kept things simple and authentic, and it made her stand out when she explained to doctors why they should use a particular medication. It was a tough job, trying to beat 20 other reps to doctors' doors at 7 in the morning to sell them drugs. Working with some innovative medicine for the treatment of AIDS, when doctors were still trying different approaches, was one experience that was to colour her working life.

Returning from Canada a few years later, another friend called to tell her of a marketing position at IDIS World Medicine. IDIS was sourcing drugs, still unlicenced in the UK, but licenced elsewhere, for particular patients in desperate need. At the interview, Natalie had an explosion of inspiration, seeing the potential of the company if it started to work with the pharma companies. It was a small outfit with only half a million turnover and before long, the owners asked her to head up sales.

She put her ideas into action, setting up a focus group, inviting 15 MDs of British pharma companies to listen to her pitch. Natalie was terrified but had taught herself to roll with fear if a job is worth doing. One man looked at her and announced, 'If anyone in my company worked with you on this, I would fire them.' This was her light-bulb moment, she says. Natalie decided not being able to see the potential was his problem and persevered until they worked with the top 20 global pharma companies. She also developed a route for hospitals to have these drugs and they set up in France, India and the US. She is immensely proud of what they achieved for pharma and patients.

By 2005, Natalie became one of the first women to win equity finance and complete a management buyout. She knew nothing of private equity, but her track record was good and all the banks and equity companies wanted in on the deal. She brought commercial thinking and strategy to the table. Under her leadership, the company re-founded from being a family company into a global one. In the years that followed, she built it to £150m turnover, with a £20m profit. IDIS was sold for £220m in 2005.

Back in the UK, Natalie was invited to turn around Healthcare at Home, Britain's largest clinical homecare business, which she achieved with huge success.

Natalie then lived in Switzerland for six years before returning to the US permanently.

Today, Natalie is chairman of her own boutique investment and management consultancy, Lucidity LLC. She advises and invests in healthcare and technology companies across Europe and the US. Natalie has also co-founded RareiTi. She had not planned to do a pharma start-up, but found she was bored, with energy to spare, and kept seeing the gaps in the market and felt compelled to provide a solution. With Lucidity, she is putting faith and money into others, whereas with RareiTi, she describes it as building with Lego again.

There are tens of millions of people suffering from incurable or undiagnosed conditions and RareiTi helps them gain access to drugs and treatments. In turn, the drug companies are encouraged to try treatments outside clinical trials and glean essential data. Ten per cent of all profits go to patient advocacy groups, which help provide a vital route between patients, drug companies and RareiTi.

Natalie's definition of personal success: *'I know what success looks like for me but am not fully there yet. I am content with my achievements personally and in my career. But in the next 10 years, I would like to do something amazing with healthcare, probably in India. I still have that creative curiosity.'*

WHEN TO MOVE ON OR UP

Natalie mentors many entrepreneurs in tech and pharma. She says that once people achieve the 1m or so mark, they get easily distracted. They have had one good idea, done some business and they then have another idea and run with this as well. But they make the critical error of forgetting they need to sell to maintain their original company. She believes that most businesses that fail are quite simply not good businesses. All too often, the model is not profitable from the start. This problem is especially prevalent in tech, where founders get investment very early, so never focus on profit. The reality is that a good business is all about the bottom line. When you start to scale, you should be demonstrating that sound bottom line or, at worst, be very close to it.

The secret to success is to do what you do well. Do not be tempted to dilute your efforts or get distracted. Business owners who secure funding too early haven't had to learn how to build a profitable business. The right way to do that is like building with Lego, putting together the pieces to make solid foundations that you can then build on.

Natalie believes that if you focus on profit all through the journey of 1–5m turnover, then you can probably run a profitable business with a 200m turnover because you will have built your skill set. When Natalie did the turnaround for Healthcare at Home, it was a massive, multi-site operation, with inadequate technology and poor leadership. On her first day, she went into the warehouse and could see what a mess it was. She found 50 people who were exceptional at what they did and told them, 'We are going to piece this together, we need a plan and seven KPIs maximum to get us up and running.' She was transparent with staff and customers alike. The rest of the teams followed and they asked the clients for 12 weeks' grace. Natalie turned it round in eight – you can't do that without knowing the basics.

When you reach 1m, you hear a lot about 'working on the business, not in it'. Natalie warns of the dangers of letting go too much at this stage. She believes it to be too early, and if you let go too much, everything will fall apart. You need to have the right people around you first.

This is also a point when you may be working with investors for the first time and that can be very tough. Some investors want to change businesses to suit them, rather than to suit the market. Natalie warns that the process of valuation is all one-sided. There can be small print in the shareholders' agreements that you may not see. Some you do, such as good and bad leavers' agreements, but you never imagine the 'bad leaver' could be you. At this stage, everyone is so friendly to you, but there are always consequences of taking money.

While money may be more readily available, it isn't easy to find people who will genuinely support you and stay with you on the journey.

Women still have a bigger battle in investment. When she raised equity funds to complete the management buyout on IDIS, Natalie was working on the press release with a PR company. She was one of the first women to raise mid-level private equity. In among the questions, the journalist fact-checked that Viagra had been one of the many drugs IDIS had imported pre-licence. To Natalie's disgust, the headlines ended up as 'Viagra importer sells to...' It was 2005, but being one of the first women to achieve an equity deal at that level was apparently of no interest to the business world.

During her time at IDIS, Natalie went from MD to CEO. The investors said they could see that she had been doing that job already. She had worked her way up to it. Natalie gets frustrated with people calling themselves CEO too early or because they have a good idea or have founded a business. She points out that a pilot needs to train before he can fly your plane. Being a CEO is the same. You should never do it without earning it, building up the required skill set. Those 10,000 hours earn you the stripes.

The skills needed when you scale up are very different and the transition isn't easy. More bureaucrats become involved and it can become boring. Many egos are floating around. The founder has to learn to let go. Natalie says the right moment for that is when they stop loving what they are doing and when they are surrounded by the right people who have got the experience. It can be difficult to let go and to figure out who to let go to, but the right people can help you see it is time to move on.

Natalie says that investors sometimes make the wrong person CEO because it looks good when raising the money. Only some people have the ability or even want to grow into a CEO role. She says we have to stop calling founders CEO and that the temptation to do so will only stop when the sheer genius of founders is appreciated. Founders are hugely important but not necessarily right to manage the next step and definitely not right if they haven't earned their stripes by doing the building work brick by brick.

When investors decide to bring in their own CEO or to sell, it is all too easy for the founder to be left utterly floored and feeling a total failure. While some escape in time, many people get hit by this concept of 'failure', which can strike hard and send them into crisis. Natalie feels strongly that founders should receive support during the hard transition of moving on.

Another mistake people make is that they form the company round them centrally. Natalie is a fan of the growth of co-founded businesses that is happening, not least because there is less focus on one person. She advises people to do things with other people from the start.

Natalie believes good leadership comes from a series of skills. If you want to do something badly enough, being very motivated and focused is easy and this enables you to overcome barriers. You have to assess things fast, to see if it is of interest and if not, park it. You have to lead from the front, show people the way and convince those around you to come too, be it staff or investors. That takes authenticity and bravery. When people ask you if something is going to work, say yes, but take the first step yourself.

Key takeaways:

- Go into investment with your eyes wide open;
- Don't confuse the skills needed to be a founder with those needed to be a CEO;
- Learn how to build a company before you run.

29

Adding Value with Vertical Integration
Jeff Fenster, Everbowl

JEFF'S STORY

Jeff Fenster is both founder and CEO of Everbowl, the superfood chain that is sweeping through California and Arizona. At age 30, he was named as a top 100 Entrepreneur in America under 35. By 37, he was in the top 100 Movers and Shakers, and a finalist for CEO of the Year. He is a serial entrepreneur with a disruptive trademark.

Jeff's father was a doctor and his mother a teacher. His aunt died of breast cancer when he was a child. He remembers asking his dad why it happened and hearing the disease had been found too late. Jeff told me that it left him with a real fear of cancer, verging on being a hypochondriac. As he grew up, he battled against that by starting to learn about nutrition.

Jeff attended the University of Arizona to obtain a BS in regional development and minor in law. He studied law at Thomas Jefferson School of Law. A year as a certified intern at the San Diego Public Defender's office followed, but a legal career was never the end goal. He was thinking of becoming a sports agent, but by this time, he was engaged, had his first daughter and didn't want to always be travelling.

Jeff changed direction and went to work as an account manager for a payroll provider called ADP. Within six months, he was the top performer. It was January then and Jeff needed his bonus badly to pay the mortgage and provide for his new daughter. He went and asked his boss for it, only to be told that it would not be paid until June. Jeff told his boss that he would leave if he didn't get it, fully expecting his boss to give way. When this didn't happen, Jeff went home and asked his fiancée what she thought about him leaving. She told him to go ahead.

He and a partner founded i-Chex, a payroll and human resources firm that later became Canopy HR. Jeff was confident in his sales abilities, but had no idea how to process payroll. It was 2007 and the Internet was still in its relative infancy so he typed the question into Google and went from there. He had another business idea for an online platform matching expanding companies to investors, but it needed funding. At that time, equity crowdfunding was illegal in the US. This was an ancient law aimed at protecting people from financial predators. However, the Internet had opened the feasibility of setting up crowdfunded equity funding so people could invest tiny amounts that they could afford to lose. Passionate that the law should be changed, Jeff co-founded Equity Circle to fight to make that happen. The campaign for legalization succeeded, though that particular platform didn't, which taught him a great deal.

Jeff and I talked about how the fear of failure holds so many back in business. His view is that fear is natural and everyone has it. He told me that when he opened his first Everbowl store, no one, not even a friend, walked in the door for the first three hours. Then one man came in, looked at the menu and went to the counter to ask, 'Can you make me bacon and eggs?' At that moment, Jeff froze, terrified and questioning what on earth he had done. But he points out that fear is not real, it is just an emotion. If you think of fear, think of a toddler: how they try and fall, try and fall, before they stand up and walk.

Jeff tells his daughter when she struggles with her maths, 'If you knew you would fail seven times and then succeed, you would fail really fast.' Jeff believes that fear is healthy; only when you become obsessed with it does it becomes paralyzing. You should see failure as part of learning, but quitting is a real failure.

Another thing he learned is to understand that there are different types of entrepreneurs and many people fail at business because they don't understand which one they are. 'Think of it like being a doctor,' he told me. 'Ask what kind of doctor you are. If I have a heart condition and you are not a heart doctor, I wouldn't choose to be treated by you.' There are start-up entrepreneurs who start a business and stay with that one business. Then there are serial entrepreneurs like Jeff, who are very good at starting new companies but no good at keeping them going past a certain point. And then there are the entrepreneur CEOs who come in once the company is up and running, and run and build it from there. Most people starting businesses will need a CEO-type entrepreneur to come in at some stage.

Once you have that clarity of who you are, your chances of success increase massively. Jeff says many people are attracted to being 'an entrepreneur and being successful' now. They see it as if it were the same as being a movie star. But then if you are an actor, you may be a YouTube star or a theatre or movie star – you need to clarify that identity.

While campaigning to legalize crowdfunding, Jeff continued opening other businesses: a recruiting company specializing in engineering and aeronautics, and JFEN Holdings, aimed at helping brands to increase their online revenue from $10 to $50 million.

By 2016, he says he wasn't doing very much and so was driving his wife and daughters crazy. His eldest daughter was three and getting her to eat vegetables was a constant fight. One evening, Jeff was battling with her to eat her courgettes but all she wanted was Cool Whip imitation cream. Eventually, he had had enough. Without much pause for thought, he tipped the Cool Whip over the courgettes and mixed the two in together. It was a huge success. The result started Jeff thinking about making really fun things to eat out of fruit and veggies and this ultimately became Everbowl, which first opened in Southern California and spread out quickly through the county and into neighbouring Arizona.

When I spoke to Jeff, they had just added a franchise option to fuel their expansion plans. The aim is to go nationwide and make superfoods available to all. Everbowl is leading the way in quick-serve restaurants, also selling their own products and offering outside catering. The superfoods are açai-based, a market that has been around for a little while but is fast heating up. Unlike most açai bowls, they don't add sugar. Instead, they offer honey and bee pollen, but otherwise, everything is vegan. Jeff is passionate about healthy eating. He believes he has overcome the objections to this lifestyle choice by offering affordable superfoods that fill people up and taste good.

There are specific patterns and traits to Jeff's start-ups that result in him dominating that market. He believes employees are any company's greatest asset and he works hard on the fun aspect of a company and its culture. His primary business principle is making friends and having fun.

Jeff is now an entrepreneur instructor at Forbes School of Business & Technology and spends an increasing amount of time speaking, which he gets enormous enjoyment from. He has a few other business ideas brewing, but likes to stay in a company for three to five years and let a CEO take it to the next level. It was a real privilege talking to Jeff, who is so full of knowledge and so downright nice.

> **Jeff's definition of personal success:** *'To me, it means having the freedom to live life on my own terms. It means maximizing my potential and being my best self. This happens through understanding your personal why and then making decisions that support that why.'*

ADDING VALUE TO YOUR COMPANY WITH VERTICAL INTEGRATION

Jeff always starts growing any business by researching market gaps and how he could disrupt that particular market. If the offering is not new, it will stagnate in time and go downhill. But there is a standout signature that makes him successful over a wide variety of different sectors. In his early career, he says that he didn't realize there was a name for his approach. In fact, it is called vertical integration. The exact definition of this is when a company also owns one or more of its supply chain companies. Jeff fell on to the idea when he was selling to payroll clients. He could see that the more staff his clients had, the more money he would make, but there was a problem. His clients had people leaving, and there was a talent shortage, so Jeff also started a recruitment company. This style takes the solution-based selling principle one step further.

Jeff explains that start-ups make the mistake of focusing on a problem and how to solve it. He teaches people to look at the problem and decide if it should be resolved or eliminated. You can often remove a problem by making a disruptive change. Jeff says a simple example is that people buy cologne because they don't want to smell of smoke – they see this as solving a problem. In Jeff's view, it isn't a problem that needs solving, but one that wouldn't exist if they stopped smoking.

With Everbowl, there are multiple-examples of vertical integration. Jeff realized that he would be building large numbers of outlets and so to do that at the most effective cost, he needed to get the price of the outlets down. He had two options: squeeze a contractor or build them himself. So, he founded WeBuild Stuff.

Similarly, Everbowl needs to buy massive quantities of coffee, so SuperFuel Coffee came into being. Getting supplies of the superfoods themselves for the chain meant copious amounts of money would go to intermediaries. Real Happy Foods, a superfood importer, was then created.

Jeff is quick to point out that you should not apply this solution everywhere. Successful vertical integration is only effective for the things you do or buy again and again. For example, he only needs one computer so there would be no point in him creating a computer company. Jeff has a natural ability to step back and simplify concepts – his brain simply doesn't get caught up in all the red herrings. Hence the solution was clear to him with his daughter of merely adding the Cool Whip to the courgettes.

Jeff was talking to a young real estate company recently. They were creating a vast amount of marketing content but even so, could not afford to create as much as they needed to build their brand. They had 21 people, all paying a vendor to create content. To him, the answer was simple: you set up a small content-providing company that either you personally or the company owns. The costs drop, the profits go up, the value of your company goes up and your problem disappears. This increases sales, increases efficiency and is a superpower in scaling businesses.

Key takeaways:

- Remember the fear of failure is natural, but never let it stop you;
- Stand back from the problem and see if the solution is to eliminate, not solve;
- Consider how often you are using a particular item before worrying about it.

30

Acquisitions and Exit Readiness

Jeremy Harbour, The Harbour Club &
Unity Group

JEREMY'S STORY

My first contact with Jeremy Harbour was when he and a group of other investors became interested in buying my business. After many discussions, Jeremy suggested that he and I build it up together to sell. I am, luckily, not too given to regret, but looking back on my decision to turn him down, I can safely say that I was a complete idiot. Quite apart from anything else, I would have learned the most fantastic amount.

One of the leading experts on mergers and acquisitions, Jeremy has advised Parliament and Buckingham Palace on business and enterprise. He is a three-time runner-up for Coutts Entrepreneur of the Year and has written columns for the *FT*, *The Sunday Times* and The Money Channel. He divides his time between his homes in Singapore and Mallorca.

Jeremy was brought up in Dorset, attending Clayesmore School. At the age of seven, he was showing entrepreneurial promise, removing his mum's flowers from the bottom of their garden, putting them in jam jars and then selling them to customers at her beauty salon. At 10, his father lost his farming business and they were forced to sell their home and start again from scratch. By 14, Jeremy was earning money of his own, buying anything cheap in bulk wholesale and selling it off at car boot sales. Then at 15, he dropped out of school and had a market stall selling watches and jewellery. At school, Jeremy had battled mild dyslexia and found formal education to be unrewarding. What he had, from his parents, was a great work ethic. By 18, he had a fast food takeaway outlet and an amusement arcade. Both failed, which he says taught him huge lessons in failure, humility and finding out that business will also behave in unexpected ways. He had to move back in with his parents.

By 19, he had bounced back and managed to have a telecoms company, building it up to about the £1m turnover mark. He was doing all the selling, while his staff did the services. Jeremy describes himself then as 'a little shark trying to bite people at every meeting, every networking event, every journey, looking at people as potential customers and wondering how much they spent on their phone bill'. People kept approaching him to sell the business, but none of the deals on offer involved giving him any cash. Deciding this could be an opportunity to learn from, he started going to meetings and instead of selling, asked, 'Do you know a telecom company for sale?' He told me that as a result, the conversations became more interesting and people immediately wanted to buy from him. The old dating principle of playing hard to get making you more attractive, he discovered, worked in business, too. He found a distressed company, bought it for £1, adding an asset to his balance sheet in one afternoon. A few more deals and the companies together were competition for Vodafone and Orange.

Jeremy sold the business and wondered what to do, realizing that he loved buying and selling businesses but not wanting to risk his hard-earned money. He bought a lot of distressed companies over the following 18 months, paying almost nothing upfront, among them a health club and spa, an IT company, a call centre and a training company. It was a crazy period of unbelievable hours, but it paid off.

Inspired by a talk he gave at the Events Company, still only 31, Jeremy decided to form The Harbour Club, where he runs exclusive three-day boot camps for business owners who want to learn the art of growing businesses by acquisition and how to exit. The Harbour Club also helps people puts deals together. He says that all the other business events talk about the 'in your business stuff' and no one helps with where to go from that, so business owners often end up spending 20 years in their business and still know absolutely nothing about what to do next. Jeremy says he only knows about 9 per cent about business, which is about 8 per cent more than most people.

He could also see that there is a huge transition going on with large numbers of boomer-owned businesses that supply everything we consume currently having no succession plans, so that makes a huge opportunity. The Harbour Club helps some of them with deals. He also set up the Unity Group to deal with businesses over £1m pre-tax profits, but being SMEs, they are still treated as high risk and as a resulting have no liquidity. They group these companies under one umbrella to become a size that can be floated and so the companies involved release capital through shares but retain their autonomy at a much lower risk.

Jeremy has now conducted more than 100 buy and sell deals, although the actual figure is likely to be somewhat higher. He has a hotel in Bali, a land investment business in Indonesia, global investments and recently bought a bank. I asked him if he felt he had reached a pinnacle of success, but Jeremy says he feels he has only just started. Throughout, he remains as straight talking and down to earth as ever and once again, incredibly generous with his time.

Jeremy's definition of personal success: For him, success has always been lifestyle focused. *'Business owners I saw were invariably overworked and underpaid, and I wanted the reverse. In both cases I have created a lifestyle I want, living mainly in Singapore and retaining my villa and yachts in Mallorca for the summer. As an adult, you get to make those sorts of choices. I am hugely lucky to have created the wealth to live somewhere expensive, but if I lived in Thailand, Malaysia or Indonesia, I could have a paradise island for next to nothing. You have that freedom by creating a lifestyle arbitrage where you can live somewhere very cheap and have a fantastic lifestyle. I measure success by the quality of my lifestyle, so I insist on working at home. This means I have a lot of time for my young family. When I do have to be away for a month or two, the family all come too.'*

ACQUISITIONS AND EXIT READINESS

Having failed to pull off a very successful exit myself, I especially wanted to ask Jeremy more about this little-talked-about aspect of business. For anyone who is not tied into deals that have involved pre-committed exit plans, this area is something people do not know enough about. Everything shared in this section is his invaluable advice and told as Jeremy told me.

Most people start businesses wanting more time and more money, or because they are fed up with someone telling them what to do. Then they find they have no time, no money, never switch off and while it's exciting for a time, in the end, it grinds you down. They don't plan long term, instead they get stuck being a glorified employee – for all it may say CEO on the business card. However, if, for example, they are the primary salesperson, it should read salesperson/CEO or engineer/CEO or whatever they mainly do. If you let that situation continue, one day you will run out of steam.

Jeremy always tests entrepreneurs to find out where they are by asking what they do all day. If they say they are having meetings about systems or sales, he knows they are still in day-to-day mode. What they should be doing, he says, is having meetings about mergers, joint ventures, acquisitions and exits.

Too many people look at wealth in the same way as traditional retirement, i.e., work your butt off until you are almost dead and then try and do what you want to do when you are hobbling around. And they approach being in business in the same way, thinking, 'I will do this for 20, 40 years and then sell.' Rather than go this route, you would do far better to do short bursts, sell a business, create capital and get back some of that time you spent on a beach thinking about your company, returned in the form of sitting on a beach not thinking about it. Tim Ferriss, in his book, *The 4-Hour Work Week*, talks about sabbaticals where you learn to tango, kickbox or be a monk for a year and then have another go at business. Once you have some time and money, you *can* buy different companies and do different things.

As soon as you are delivering a product or service efficiently, many believe that all those business needs can be serviced by jobs. It is simply not true, it has to be you. You need to systemize it and focus on value building, even if you are not planning to sell immediately. Anyone should start this somewhere between 500k and 1m turnover depending on the sector. By that time, many entrepreneurs are bored by the day-to-day after the excitement of building it.

You have to make the shift from business runner to business owner. If you don't, it results in a Groundhog Day situation. This is also a core component if you do want to sell one day. One of the major issues is people say, 'No one can do it as well as me' or 'Without me, it will be a disaster,' and wonder who on earth they could ever get to run it for them.

Jeremy says this does appear to be a real issue. In his experience, most CEOs and MDs he has considered are a) only available because there is something wrong with them or b) their CV says they are good at what you want, but that means they have done it before – perhaps built a business from 1–10 million – in which case, they will be looking for a new challenge, not to mention the fact that in some cases the last company will have had the best of them.

So, where do you find a young, engaging paragon who knows how to run a business like yours and is still hungry enough to build it up? The answer is that you find them in a business very similar to yours, but one that already has an MD in place. They might be competitors, people you slightly envy or even hate because you lose business to them. So, you suggest a merger. With a merger, everyone wants to run it. You pretend you do too and use it as a massive negotiating lever. You will end up becoming a major shareholder and a non-exec with an exceptional shareholders agreement protecting you. The new joint CEO will relish the challenge and opportunity of running both. You have your time back, no staff or customers to bother about and can indeed focus on mergers, acquisitions, everything to build value – best of all, you get to exit, leaving them in place as CEO.

Jeremy says that most people are inexperienced in deals and so when they start to think about what comes next, they are completely out of their depth. He advises that you start practising, even if you have no immediate plans of selling. Try some tactical acquisitions that add value on products, services or geographical differential. Or just buy a distressed company for £1, give it some help on costs until it looks a bit better and practise going through the selling process. Practising like this will provide you with the experience and confidence that will show when you do a big deal to exit.

Not understanding deal structures and how deals are done is the biggest barrier to people selling successfully. Often, they rely too heavily on professional advisors. These fall into two categories: the fee takers, who run up massive amounts of hours and take ages to get anything done, and the brokers, who are incentivized to get people to sign up with them, but don't add much to the deal.

The most important thing is to have an outstandingly good information memorandum, the 'brochure' for your business, with all the financial analysis, competitor analysis, market share. Brokers don't put that together. You also need to have a one-page executive summary, which is a one-page teaser for your business. Once you have got those, simply advertise it on a businesses for sale site, for the minimal cost of an advertisement. Advertising, plus some filtering of the results, is what the broker would have done, but this way, you have all the control and minimum outlay.

Prepare your due diligence. Due diligence questionnaires are easy to find and download from the net. Create a Dropbox or Google Doc with all the documents in, so it looks professional and gives the best impression that you know what you are doing and that your business is well run. Then you can invite people in to have access.

Be ready with any finance needed, either by bank finance or private lender, and expect to be flexible on how you will get paid. You may want a million, but no one is going to pay you that on day one. They will want to see some transactions, some consistency, so be prepared. It is never as much about the price as it is about the structure of the deal. You have to go with the structure that feels comfortable to you.

Advisors, Jeremy says, just argue they will get you more cash than anyone else and instead put off good potential buyers by being ridiculous over the whole process. Of course, the first time, you will make mistakes. That is why practice is such a good idea, but Jeremy is clear that his biggest mistake was ever using advisors.

Key takeaways:

- From 500k turnover upwards, start prepping your business to sell, irrespective of whether you have a plan to exit at any point;
- Negotiate the transition from working in the business to working on it;
- Practise buying and selling companies to add to your bottom line.

PART SEVEN

Success

WHAT SUCCESS LOOKS LIKE

Before we sum up how to get there, I wanted to take a brief moment to sum up what I have learned about how people are defining success. Listening to start-up founders over the years, the reasons they want their own business tend to fall into distinct categories. Some people are looking to provide for their families, others for a more balanced lifestyle. Some are looking for freedom, while some want to be mega-rich.

Over the course of researching this book specifically, I talked to many, many established and successful entrepreneurs. While there are similarities in their reasons for doing what they do, having attained success, they all dismiss financial motivation. When I query this, they qualify that money enables some of what they define success as. What money helps buy is freedom – freedom to do the things in life that you want to do, both at work and personally, and freedom comes out clearly as the top motivator and measurement for success.

Alongside that is a need to feel good about what we do at work. People often talk about wanting to have done their job well, working hard, doing things right, doing something they are proud of. Doing work that makes them happy is a must because life is too short not to be.

Most people describe that satisfaction in terms of how they impact others. This impact is easy to identify with the entrepreneurs who specifically tackle society's issues, from poverty to injustice, such as Dame Shellie Hunt, James Bartle and Durell Coleman. But even within everyday business life, making a useful contribution to their customers' daily lives and giving them good service matters to these successful entrepreneurs. Many also talk about helping others on an individual basis. Taking pleasure in developing their teams has also been a constant source of satisfaction, from Stephen Kelly's experiences at Oracle, Adrian Kingwell's Book of Life theory, or the inventive ways of making working life fun under Rob Hamilton at Instant Offices.

Being able to choose who you work with is another privilege success brings. In return, creating a company where people want to work is a small price to pay.

A major benefit of financial success is achieving a great balanced lifestyle. No one I spoke to defined this in terms of fast cars and executive jets, but as having the time to spend with family, a balance of work and home, and time to be grateful for the present.

I hear more and more voices saying that happiness and success lies in self-development and in finding a purpose, that personal North Star. These successful people want to feel they have become the best version of themselves and created a legacy that has improved other people's lives for the better in some way.

To me, it signals the growth of a much more meaningful reason for businesses in the future that can only benefit humanity.

31

A Summary of Advice

SUMMARY

One of the first points that came up a lot when I was interviewing for this book was that everyone should take advice under a 'buyer beware' warning. Everyone is different and their circumstances and businesses are, too. That said, overall, some strong themes are repeated time and again, regardless of sectors or demographics.

The consensus is that scaling your business is not for everyone and you should never, ever do so without good reason and unless you are scale-ready. When you increase from that first million into the multis, you will need to make changes to both yourself and the business. Don't drift into it, expecting all will be well by doing more of the same things that you have always done.

Taking time to plan the scale is critical. You need the right structures in place, from digitalizing to systemizing each process. You will need help in these new waters. Approach advisors and mentors. Write to them and ask for help in their specific areas of expertise. Many will be happy to give you the benefit of their experience.

Assess your team. Who you have on board now will be crucial to your success. Are they growth-ready and do they buy into the idea? Do they want the changes growth will bring, or do you need to bring on board people who do?

You will also be carving out a more definitive position in the market and defining the problem you are solving. If either of those are wrong, you will not succeed. The overall strength of the market you are aiming to grow in is critical. Study that marketplace and decide if there is plenty of room, if it is buoyant and if it has unmet needs. If you are looking at different areas globally, research, establish a presence and review what you offer to suit each market. Everywhere, look for those gaps the competition isn't meeting, which your customers tell you about. Stick to what you do best and stay true to the customers you know best. Base your plans on what they tell you.

Funding is the topic that most divides opinion. There has been a shift to venture capital funding start-ups and with technology businesses, in particular, winning large amounts of funding. This shift has also led to the rapid growth in the numbers of incubators and accelerators. Accelerators are especially useful for contacts.

Many seasoned entrepreneurs I spoke to warn of the high failure rates, the over-valuations, the illusion of successful businesses that don't make a profit and entrepreneurs who may not have had any experience in building a company from the bottom up.

The majority of people I asked about this agreed – don't borrow unless you absolutely have to. If you decide to, then plan well ahead. Crowdfunding can be a sound method, but it still takes one to two years to research thoroughly. If you are going for Angels' or VCs' funding, use an expert advisor and always over-research. I heard terrible stories about VCs, though I'm not suggesting that everyone has a bad experience. However, everyone did agree that VC funding means accepting your business is no longer your baby and that, at some stage, it will be sold, possibly without your agreement.

Your team will make or break your business. You can have the best concept, the perfect customers, but you are on the road to nowhere without the right team. If you have a strong vision or purpose and only recruit people in tune with that, you are a good step on the way there.

Once you have a team, you need to be open and transparent, sharing not just the vision but also the plan. Pay fair, though not overboard, but make it fun and help your team to reach individual goals. Look out for the rotten apples and remove them fast. Their toxic effect can destroy a whole team. Be an authentic leader and lead from the front.

Talking to customers comes first, middle and last. Only by talking to them continually can you completely nail and understand your buyers' personae. Tech can help, but it is not enough on its own. You and everyone on the team need to talk and listen to the customers to understand their needs, their problems. Always be authentic with your customers and continually think of how best to serve them. Give to them, be it great content or additional experiences and opportunities. Don't demand personal information in return. Use tech to optimize your customer journey, but never forget that making the journey a memorable experience for your customer is what's going to count. Nail the metrics and optimize your acquisition model. Find salespeople who know and love your market, who are emotionally resilient to rejection and who will listen more than they talk. Sell honestly and authentically.

It is all too easy to lose sight of the fact that a business's purpose is to make money and have the ability to continue to do that sustainably. It is also easy to focus on growth or be distracted by firefighting, but no profit means no business at some future point. Creating value will keep you afloat, make you appeal more to investors and make you more saleable. And while you may believe you will never sell, something drastic and unforeseen might happen to change that. Always be prepared. Learn to build value. Get expert advice on procurement, ensuring value, quality and continuation. Evaluate high-value suppliers and see if you could service that supply better with a second small business. Making your business robust and stable at this stage means you can scale later to whatever size the market can bear.

One other point people disagreed upon is to what degree at £1m turnover you should be working *in* or working *on* the business: that famous distinction made by Michael Gerber in his book *The E-Myth*. Some think it is crucial to be working 'on' already while others felt it was too soon. I suspect it is sector dependent and individual business dependent. While moving to working 'on' will become essential at some point, only attempt it if your business is ready and a lot of that will depend on your management team. They have to be in place for you to step out and some scaling may be necessary to pay for that team to be good enough.

Scaling isn't for everyone. For one thing, it may be pointless. If you have a great little business that is making a substantial profit, ask yourself why you are considering it. It is tempting to buy into the idea that all growth is good. However, not only is this not true, but there is also an enormous risk that it could destroy your business.

It is just starting to be better understood how mentally tough you need to be as a leader. You will need personal resilience and a great support team to see you through tough times. Accept that failure is part of learning, but don't let fear stop you. You will need commitment, a strong desire to learn and focus, focus, focus.

Be clear on why you are doing this, what your purpose is, whom you impact, what that North Star is. Check that all those things will be served best by scaling up and if so, then use that passion to bring the momentum needed to get you there.

Acknowledgements

The most enormous thanks goes to the entrepreneurs in this book: James Bartle, Bev Hurley, Stephen Kelly, Durell Coleman, Nicole Lamond, Alex Packham, Ben Revell, Russell Dalgleish, David Siegel, Roby Sharon-Zipser, Dame Shellie Hunt, Ranzie Anthony, Rob Hamilton, Natalie Lewis, Adrian Kingwell, David Meerman Scott, George Sullivan, Matt Sweetwood, Ed Molyneux, Paris Cutler, Andrew Milbourn, Anneke van den Broek, James Davidson, Sam Kennis, Simon Wadsworth, Lex Deak, Mike Lander, Natalie Douglas, Jeff Fenster and Jeremy Harbour.

Between you all, you made me laugh a lot, cry occasionally, become a great deal wiser and remain in constant awe of your achievements.

Sadly too many to mention, there is an even longer list of lovely people who help those mentioned above, be it as PAs or PRs, who helped me out in liaising back and forth. They were all hugely kind and patient.

Also, on the kind and patient list, has to be Matt James, assistant editor at Bloomsbury Business. Not only did he encourage me with my submission, but he has tolerated a barrage of questions over several months. Thanks to him and everyone at Bloomsbury.

A final thank you too goes to Kate Bassett (now at *Management Today*) and Hunter Ruthven, now at *Be the Business*, both of whom were my editors at *Real Business*, Kate briefly and Hunter for many years. His encouragement of my writing meant the world to me and without him I would never have arrived at this point.

Index